Harry Armfield works in the advertising industry. He is the author of a previous style book, *Cool*.

By the same author

Cool

HARRY ARMFIELD

Status

GRAFTON BOOKS

A Division of the Collins Publishing Group

LONDON GLASGOW
TORONTO SYDNEY AUCKLAND

Grafton Books
A Division of the Collins Publishing Group
8 Grafton Street, London W1X 3LA

A Grafton Paperback Original 1990

A CIP catalogue record for this book is available
from the British Library

ISBN 0-586-21066-0

Printed and bound in Great Britain by
Collins, Glasgow

Set in Times

CONTENTS

ACKNOWLEDGEMENTS

The author would like to thank the following for their invaluable support and assistance in putting this book together:

Pierre Barnes, Hugo Tightwad de Danzig, the Soton Eye, the Ellsworth-Smiths, the Nitch-Smiths, Mike Williams, Anthony and Judith Larcombe, Clive Steer, Group Captain 'Badger' Bajzert, Peter and Paul Productions, the Cambridge Pieronis, Michael and Jeanette, Annie and Rombo Sullivan, Sonya Shields QC, John Walsh, Carolyn Hart, Philip Kerr, Lisa Jenkins, Jane Searle, Rob Pugh, Anthony and 'Fungie' Barnes, Joanna Rowley, Laurence and Polly Leg-Meadow, Bernadette Bout, Mr and Mrs A, Camilla June, Catherine Mellor, Bob Lett and of course Paula.

Thanks also to Rex Features Ltd and Ferrari for permission to reproduce illustrations.

A CAUTIONARY TALE

A man goes to visit an old friend whom he hasn't seen for years. They were at school together and highly competitive both academically and on the sporting field. Even though the man hasn't seen the old friend for some time, he has followed his high-flying career and general success with much interest, since in many ways it reflects his own career and success. Both men like to think they have a lot of status in their respective societies.

The man is surprised at the relative ordinariness of his old friend's home as his wife ushers him into the living room and leaves him to call her husband. The man is shocked to find that the living room furnishings are very naff indeed, if not a fraction vulgar. While awaiting his friend, a nifty foot flipped under the carpet edge reveals a label that confirms it is indeed from Allied Carpets. The man can hardly conceal his delight at discovering a symbol of his old friend's debased status. The competitive urge returns once again. The man intends pointing out his observations as soon as he and his old friend have met, so he can for once and for all establish his superiority.

The old friend enters the room, they shake hands and before any further conversation takes place, the man wryly comments: 'Nice carpet.'

The old friend looks a little bemused, but confirms what the man is dying to hear: 'It's from Allied Carpets, actually.'

'Really,' replies the man. 'I bought my living room carpet on a recent trip to Bodrum. It's Turkish antique, you know.'

At this point, though a seemingly innocent exchange of information has taken place with regard to an everyday item such as a carpet, the man has in fact already introduced several avenues of status superiority. By informing the old friend he bought his carpet in Turkey, he is really saying that: (a) he has international status since he travels further than Dorking to buy his carpets; (b) he has status because he has the style to find something a little more elusive than a mass produced item; (c) he has status because 'money is no object'; (d) he has introduced what is known as 'conversational status', the ability to subtly demonstrate a sense of one-upmanship with the smallest, most casual of remarks.

It would seem that the man, with one casual but intentional remark, is one move away from checkmate in this particular status chess game. It would seem that victory is but a white square away, when his old friend replies, 'I'm sorry, there seems to have been some misunderstanding. This is the servants' quarters. I thought you'd come about the job.'

Status, as they say, giveth and status taketh away.

STATUS: AN INTRODUCTION

As a schoolkid, the word 'status' might have sent you scurrying for the nearest *Concise Oxford*, before some bespectacled spotty swot didactically revealed to the rest of the class its Latin derivation.

As a rebellious teenager or 'Pretty Vacant' person, its mere mention might have caused you to smash your parents' favourite Johnny Mathis collection over the Chippendale, before you reluctantly agreed to join the family corporation.

Where once the word 'status' might simply have signified one half of a name generally associated with a protracted bout of headbanging, today its message and appeal comes across loudly and clearly, though it's nothing to do with heavy metal music.

In the eighties there was an obsessive across-the-board desire for that which was once the province of 'class-conscious aesthetes' of the Aldous Huxley variety or the 'Keep-up-with-the-Jones' clones. Now that which sets you apart from the rest, that which places you above the seething rabble, that which elicits hunched scowls of jealousy in the wake of your rising star and gleaming tooth, that which bestows on you special thingies that other people simply can't have, is once again popular. Serious stuff. Essential. A *sine qua non*, no less.

Money and power are once again fashionable. The Bank Generation has replaced the Blank Generation. Competition is rife, and despite occasional mystifying aberrations such as marbled denim and the inexplicable popularity of yellow beer, fewer and fewer folk wish to be part of the crowd. Everyone wants to be a noble brow ahead of the next pushy sod.

Status is difficult to define

Status comes in many forms, many of which are easily identifiable, and many of which, more often than not, are universally recognized. For example, where you live, how you live and whom you live with is often a reasonable guide to your status. As is how you make your money, and what you spend it on. Where you go and how you get there is also a common indicator of status. As is what you eat, where you eat, and how you eat it. Status could easily be the names you drop, and the names you keep. The things you say and in how many languages. And though status can be international, we also expect it to be parochial and to be able to cross frontiers.

Yet within all these general categories which are all perfectly adequate guides to status, more or less every individual, every social division, has a different view of status, a different way of gauging it, a different set of rules. And, as if the subject wasn't already complicated enough, the problem is further complicated by the fact that any view of status will vary with age, sex, class and nationality. It's just as well status is a complicated subject though. If it were a simple, straightforward matter, there'd be no fun in scoring points off someone else.

The *Shorter Oxford English Dictionary* tells us that status relates to your 'position or standing in society'. But since there are usually two societies in this and many other countries – that society which we are all a member of, and that society specifically reserved for dukes and oils, etc. – the definition has already become more convoluted.

The *New Collins Concise English Dictionary* offers a concise definition. Status is 'the relative position or standing of a person or thing', whereas a status symbol is 'a possession which is regarded as proof of the owner's social position, wealth, prestige, etc.'. Whichever way you look at it it's all relative. The Collins view is apposite, but it still doesn't take into account the subtleties of status.

For example, no one would deny that a sergeant's rank carries higher status than a private's, that it is better to be employed than unemployed, and that having more money carries more status than less money. But Elvis Presley was once a private in the

American Army and undoubtedly had more status internationally than his company sergeant.

Joey Boswell of *Bread* soap opera fame is unemployed, but still manages to drive a Mark 2 Jaguar, a classic status car. And most people have less money than Ferdinand and Imelda Marcos had, but twice as much status (after all, would you have invited them to your dinner party if you had had the chance?). So it's impossible to generalize when it comes to status. Every case must be judged on its merits and thoroughly explored.

Inverted Status

A further complication. Today status covers much more than the traditional big wads, titles and success in business. Though these are all significant aspects of status today, the subject has since refined itself, expanded and become more diversified. Nowadays status is manifested with greater subtlety. Things have also become more complicated, and 'inverted status' can carry as much clout, if not more, than ordinary status.

Whereas Goldsmith and Maxwell may sue the last pair of Y-fronts off *Private Eye* for being pilloried in such an odious, scandalous rag, there are many other completely sane people who would sell their grandmothers into slavery just to appear in *Street of Shame*, *Grovel*, *Pseuds' Corner* and *White Shit of the Year Award*.

For every Cabinet Minister and head of state that cringes and whimpers, as their *Spitting Image* puppet appears emaciated and slavering, week after week, on the box, there are hundreds who consider that having your effigy on TV in the form of a spitting image, rather than being detrimental to your reputation, is instead a great honour. Despite being publicly hung drawn and quartered across the Wiltons of a million living rooms up and down the country, satirized subjects are at least considered worthy of ridicule; worthy, therefore, of attention. In fact, it has been known for those in the public eye to get quite upset if their spitting image is subsequently dropped from the show, since it is often an indication of a drop in popularity, which frequently foreshadows dismissal from the Cabinet or some other position of eminence.

The short cut to happiness

1. STATUS IS SOMETHING THAT SETS YOU APART from the riff-raff, the plebs, the hoi polloi, the scumbags (i.e. other people).

Status is something that establishes your superiority over them, often without the necessity of ever having to come into contact with them (the less the better, if you ask me). The wider the gap, the greater the status.

2. EVERYONE SECRETLY COVETS STATUS: Secretly because true status-seekers prefer to remain invisible. They aspire to it on the quiet without drawing undue attention to themselves. Once the status goal has been achieved, then and only then can you bask in its carefully filtered sunshine.

The most satisfying forms of status are those which you are perceived by others to have acquired effortlessly and without really caring one way or the other. That is what arouses interest, and that is when the green-eyed monster awakens. That's what makes everyone want to play the game: 'Crikey, he's got all that status, but he doesn't care! Now if that were me . . .'

For example the pop star constantly mobbed by the gold-top of the town's jailbait, who reveals to the pop journalist or chat show host that, quite frankly, 'This fame fing is a real drag. I'd rather be a librarian or out visiting old ladies.' Do we buy that? Of course not. They love it. They hate it. But they wouldn't be without it.

3. STATUS IS ELUSIVE: If it wasn't it would be worthless. Champagne, for example, used to be high status indeed. Now everyone drinks it by the horse-trough. Even a good vintage champagne like Louis Roederer Cristal is more likely to signify an overloaded wallet and a newly purchased *Hugh Johnson's Wine Guide* than be a status indicator. The same is true for diamonds. Too many diamonds on the market and they're considered vulgar.

It's an unfortunate fact of life that everyone wants what is elusive. Sooner or later our economic system finds a way to fulfil that demand, and the search for elusiveness must begin again.

4. IT'S NOT A PASSING PHASE, or a trend or a style. Status is a long-lasting thing, unlike the once-coveted symbols of an afghan

coat, a houseful of pine furniture and a Filofax, or the professions of DJ or air stewardess.

Once you're on the status treadmill you adapt and keep adapting, until such time as it becomes perfectly acceptable for everyone to be a bag person, play bingo, and drive a Zastava.

5. PEOPLE DON'T REQUIRE MONEY OR BREEDING TO HAVE IT: Sure it helps to be related to a Rothschild, or to be an heir, or 'Your Grace'. But think about the image of the poor struggling artist in the Parisian garret. Consider the Fulton Mackay character in the movie *Local Hero*, who lived simply and reclusively in a hut on the beach, but who commanded the respect and admiration of the whole village and later the oil billionaire who visited him, played by Burt Lancaster.

6. IT MAY BE BLINDINGLY OBVIOUS, but it's more likely to be blindingly invisible.

Status and class

In Britain the difference between the classes, the so-called class system, has been one indicator of social status that has remained fairly consistent over the centuries. Of course Britain is not alone in identifying such social divisions among the populace. Indeed many countries still have standard class divisions, if not our own upper, middle and lower, then more standard stereotypes of nobility and commoner, landowner and peasant, monied and poor. Even in a relatively young country like the United States, there is still a middle and a working class. Few would disagree, however, that probably nowhere in the world are the careful distinctions of class such a refined art as in Britain.

An exceptionally complicated facet of English life, class as an indicator of social status is only something that is truly understood by the few, even among the natives themselves. John Cleese, Ronnie Barker and Ronnie Corbett once performed a sketch on the sixties satirical show, *The Frost Report*, that came close to identifying and comparing the three separate classes. Viv Stanshall's *Sir Henry at Rawlinson End* was a brave attempt at shafting the aristocracy. Jilly Cooper made some interesting observations in her book *Class*. But so did the skinhead movement in the seventies.

There is a notion, particularly among foreigners, that each class should be a stepping stone for the next. The reality seems to be more irrational. The working class, though they would like to have more cash in their pocket, are quite happy being what and where they are. So are the upper classes. It is only the middle classes who quite like the idea of moving upward. There are exceptions: Bryan Ferry, Mick Jagger, for example. These are of the view that as you move from the lower, through the middle to the upper so your status will increase.

The only conclusion that can be drawn is that all the different classes think they're in the best class. And the different levels of status come mainly from within a particular class, with occasional forays out of it and into things which are nothing to do with class.

Working class status

A member of the working class is, more often than not, proud to be a member of the working class. He or she talks proudly of working class 'roots', and sees him or herself as the 'salt of the earth'. Many, particularly those from the north of England, frown on one of their numbers betraying their Andy Capp origins, as D. H. Lawrence's heroes did all too frequently in his novels.

While Karl Marx and Joey Boswell, of *Bread* fame, are true working class heroes, Arthur Dailey is not. Though he has 'made good' financially, he is still an oik. He is also a cockney, a breed which has long lost its status through overkill as a TV advertising sterotype. Terence Stamp, Bob Hoskins and Michael Caine, though also of the cockney breed, have all made the transformation to successful international screen and media stars, and Stamp has lost all trace of his former accent. For these types, true working class status is the ability to communicate and be on good drinking terms with members of every class, miner and earl alike.

Apart from international film star, one of the biggest status professions for this group is that of rock star. The status you get from starving in an attic before eventually making good is an ultimate dream for anyone of impoverished upbringing. And the

Beatles rather than the Rolling Stones are fondly remembered as the earliest role models for this profession.

Other popular status professions for this class include Labour Prime Minister, heavyweight boxer, First Division footballer, underworld gangleader (like the Bob Hoskins character in *The Long Good Friday*), a dealer in the City, a tabloid Editor, a left-wing university lecturer (like Howard Kirk in *The History Man*), or an alternative comedian, like Ben Elton and the *Comic Strip* brigade. Sport and sportsmen have heavy status within this social group, even if it does mean being a member of 'The Intercity Firm' (an exalted group of football hooligans).

Pastimes such as appearing on quiz shows, bingo, spotting the ball, winning the pools, eating six chicken Tikka Masalas on top of twenty-seven pints of flat lager, and still being able to get it up are all ambivalent forms of so-called working class status. Traditionally, a large percentage of this class leaves full-time education ASAP. But this is a changing phenomenon. In the same way as the Labour Party is actually split between the old ways and the new, the very left and the not so left, so too are there differences of opinion as to what constitutes working class status and what doesn't. In Thatcherite Britain, wide ownership of property (not living in a council flat) and more material things may have become more of a priority.

WORKING CLASS LITERATURE: Karl Marx, George Orwell, sociological and economic histories, D. H. Lawrence.

WORKING CLASS MOVIE DIRECTORS: Ken Loach, Derek Jarman.

WORKING CLASS TV PROGRAMMES: *Blind Date*, *East Enders*, *Dynasty*, *The Big Match*, darts and snooker.

WORKING CLASS CARS: Any Ford. A Porsche complete with spoilers and £2,000 in-car stereo. A Roller with a gold flying lady.

WORKING CLASS MUSIC: The Clash, Fine Young Cannibals.

Middle class status

The middle class are voracious consumers of books, magazines and other reading material. Newspapers will include the *Sun* and *Sunday Sport*, (as well as the upmarket dailies), even if these are excused as joke reading.

Information is what makes this class tick, what makes its members keep that precious step ahead of the next man. New trends and styles are quickly pinpointed and relentlessly pursued, till the next one comes along. This class works hard in the predominantly white-collar professions. They follow the Samuel Smiles philosophy of self-help, and believe in riches and wealth as the fruits of their hard desk-bound labours.

'Standard of living' is a key status phrase. A knighthood is the ultimate status symbol at the end of the rainbow, and a passport into the next class.

Yet status is not all in hard work. There must be a balance between the achievements of the upwardly mobile and their display of the intellectual and artistic. This may be reflected in the yuppie antics of Alex in the *Independent*, combat survival games, cellular phones, obsessions with property prices, arguments about Salman Rushdie and freedom of speech. The ultimate social expression of this class is the dinner party, or the opera. Shopping is taken very seriously, from Conran's to every other style shop in every corner of the globe. Status symbols in this class are a bit of a cliché these days since they still include the Mont Blanc pens and Rolex watches. Personal computers are to the middle class what Doc Martens were to skinheads.

MIDDLE CLASS LITERATURE: *The Bonfire of the Vanities, Which Computer*.

MIDDLE CLASS MOVIES: Mostly American. And once every five years a trip to the NFT to see an 'Art' film.

MIDDLE CLASS TV: *Fawlty Towers* repeats, *Capital City*.

MIDDLE CLASS CARS: Invariably German. Petrol: lead-free.

Upper class status

The upper class in Britain, though without land and titles, is bred to think and act like the aristocracy, and to provide it with plenty of help and chums to maintain the status quo. Every member of the upper class will know at least one or several members of the aristocracy and after a while it's impossible to tell the two apart.

If you or your parents want you to escape from your middle class or lower class origins and become part of the upper class, you have to begin at birth. The right friends, the right connections for the future, accent and breeding, all begin at birth or at nursery or prep school.

To become a member of the aristocracy, on the other hand, is nigh on impossible for a commoner (knighthoods excluded). Membership can only be inherited, unless of course you're prepared to marry one, like Grace Kelly (Princess Grace), Anthony Armstrong-Jones (Lord Snowdon), or Tracy Ward (Marchioness of Worcester). But it is possible to hobnob freely with them, especially if one is 'amusing', 'frightfully chic', or 'in the hit parade' (Mick, Bryan, Simon, Mark, etc.). One whiff of scandal, however, and the 'Uppers' instantly close ranks. If you're one of them (Fergie's dad), well and good. If you're not (Stephen Ward – Profumo scandal), tough.

Though an amusing and predominantly lighthearted read, the *Sloane Ranger's Handbook* gives as much insight into this class as fifteen years' subscription to *The Lady*. So long as you go to the right schools, make the right chums, enter the right regiments, join the right financial institutions, kill the right fox and speak through your nose instead of through your mouth, you're well on the way.

Money has to be the right kind; old money rather than new. The nouveaus are frowned upon. You don't necessarily have to own land, as long as you know how to act and behave on it.

The *Sloane Ranger's Handbook* advises them to cry when they sing Christmas carols, but not when they attend funerals. This is a crucial observation, and governs much of what the upper classes do and how they act.

It's status to read *Winnie the Pooh* and Beatrix Potter as well as the *FT*. It's status to drive a Range Rover, but cycle a beaten up old ungeared bike. It's status to appear in the social pages, especially if there's a mention of 'Melons' (Lady Helen Windsor) close by. It's status to wear Burberry, to have rooms with a view, to own some of England's green and pleasant land. To defend Queen and Country and declining values. To watch *Yes, Minister* and *To the Manor Born*. To read the *Daily Telegraph*. To live in Knightsbridge and Belgravia. To inherit a lot of money. To have a Daddy that's chairman of several multinationals. To ride to hounds. Not to have too much to do with 'lefties' ('the sixties were bad enough'). It's status to do the 'right thing'. Alan B'Stard, the *New Statesman*, is the current hero for keeping the oiks at bay.

Lower middle class status

Not the best class for status. Better not bring too much attention to your origins if you're a member of this one – 'Dad, will you please not wash the car on the same day as everyone else. Take it to a frigging carwash.' 'Forget mowing the front lawn every Sunday; grow some trees.' 'The Caravan? The brake was faulty and it went straight over a cliff. I just couldn't stop it, honest.' 'Mum, antique "reproduction" doesn't mean it's antique, you know.'

The only way this particular class can have any status at all is by making an internationally successful movie of their origins, which is about as likely as Derek Hatton winning the next election.

Car accessories are a favourite of this group, as are DIY and home improvements. Favourite shops include Halfords and B&Q. Car of the moment is a small Volvo saloon, or a seventeen-year-old immaculately preserved, never been over 30 m.p.h., regularly serviced, waxed every week, Austin Maxi. Heroes include Richard Briers in *Ever Decreasing Circles*, Delboy in *Only Fools and Horses* and Cliff Richard. The ultimate status symbol of this particular group is a little motor sailing dinghy with a name like *Ocean Wave* permanently moored down at Littlehampton.

A BRIEF HISTORY OF STATUS

The beginning of time

Initially, it was very important if you were ever going to have any status at all, to evolve into a human rather than remain an animal – though the early humans were a rather sorry lot and a dinosaur with a similar IQ seemed to have more fun.

If you glimpsed the *2001* monolith, that was certainly something to brag about at the local watering hole, especially if you were suddenly instilled with a mysterious new knowledge that enabled you to pick up a large bone and bash the brains out of your enemies.

The sapiens that invented fire probably had quite a bit of status in the tribe, as would the retard who invented the wheel. Beyond that, it was important to your status as a man to be a brave and fearless hunter, and for a woman to resemble Raquel Welch in the film *One Million Years BC*.

COVETED STATUS SYMBOLS: a large club with a spike in it. A leopard skin two piece. A set of all-purpose 'Swiss Army' flints. A cave mural by Zob the Hirsute.

Ancient Egypt

To be a member of one of the first civilizations was status indeed, even if you never reached coveted pharaoh status. The best jobs were to be had in the Royal Court, while the worst were on the building site of the Pyramids. A great sign of private status at this time was bathing in asses' milk. If Cleopatra was the particular woman on the end of your arm you had it made.

The highest form of status was probably being buried in a Great Pyramid with a pharaoh, like King Cheops. The lowest form of status was probably being buried alive in a Pyramid with a pharaoh like King Cheops.

COVETED STATUS SYMBOL: a house in Babylon with hanging gardens.

Ancient China

This was one of the more civilized civilizations. China, rather paradoxically, gave the world the wisdom of Confucius as well as that popular de-atomizer, gunpowder. High status people tended to have great amounts of land and property so a great wall around your estate was a big sign of status, since it implied you had a lot to protect. Emperor was the top job to hold, followed by acupuncturist.

COVETED STATUS SYMBOLS: thirteen-inch fingernails, a moustache trimmer, manure.

Ancient Greece

Sports and sportsmen had high status in these times. The further you could throw a discus or a javelin, the more you were showered with garlands by young virgins. But those who could run were careful not to show it, since they often ended up as a messenger boy to army generals, running double marathons and eventually dying of exhaustion. Fashions were fairly minimal fabric-wise, and if you had a good body you usually went around almost totally naked (except, that is, when visiting the temple). Not to have bonked Helen of Troy was a great sign of status in these times.

COVETED STATUS SYMBOLS: a wooden horse, a golden fleece, an Argonaut.

The time of Christ

If you were a Pharisee in this age you were doing fine, but the job that really carried real status was shepherd. It also carried far more status to be poor than rich in these times on account of how difficult it was for a rich person to pass through the eye of a needle. Other professions that carried a lot of status were prophet and apostle. But most of all it was best to be a Roman, and preferably Caesar, provided you could survive past thirty.

COVETED STATUS SYMBOLS: lots of sheep, gold, frankincense, myrrh.

Arthurian times

A Knight of the Round Table was a mucho fabuloso position to hold in Arthurian times. For, after royalty, the odd court jester and magician, there were only poor, starving peasants. Travel was one of the perks of a knight's status job. And despite the dangers, there were always plenty of fair maids and square meals available. A knight's status was reflected in the number of poems and tales that were written of his exploits. The woman to have on the end of your arm was either the shy but sensitive Lady of Shalott, or the more outgoing Guinevere; the man – Lancelot, or Gawain, the ozone-friendly Green Knight.

COVETED STATUS SYMBOLS: the Holy Grail, a chastity belt, a key to the chastity belt.

The Renaissance

Merchant, member of the Medici Court, banker or painter were the status professions to be in during the Renaissance, though if you were a painter it was very important to have patronage. It was no status whatsoever to be poor during this period or without artistic talent. Venice was the status address of the time, particularly if you had a St Mark's Square postcode. Despite the fact that she was no beauty, after Leonardo's portrait of her, Mona Lisa was definitely the gal to walk out with. Considering the high status enjoyed by the likes of Leonardo and Michelangelo, if you wanted to be considered a serious status contender it was best to have a name that ended in 'o'. Outside of Venice, it was considered high status to have the ear of Cesare Borgia, rather than vice versa.

COVETED STATUS SYMBOLS: a palazzo, a designer codpiece, a motor gondola.

Victorian Times

To be a man of property, to be wealthy, to be at least middle class or upwards, to be a complete hypocrite: these were some of the things that gave you status during the reign of Queen Victoria. It never failed to give a great status buzz when you could say to some snotty, down-and-out flea-bitten beggar, 'Here's a shilling, now be off with you.' If you were working class or poor, your only chance was to join the army and stick your neck out far enough to win a limited edition Victoria Cross – the ultimate status symbol for a soldier.

With the great superficial Puritanism of the age, surviving a scandal was not easy, so Gladstone did very well to reinterpret his visits to prostitutes as a crusade to save fallen women. Disraeli also did well to 'climb to the top of the greasy pole' (i.e. become Prime Minister). Oscar Wilde was the man to be seen with (at least during the day), Sarah Bernhardt the woman.

COVETED STATUS SYMBOLS: an empire, shares in the Suez Canal, Penny Black first day covers.

The First World War

Surviving it, with at least one limb intact, was the biggest form of status to be had at the time.

The twenties and thirties

Much of the status for these two decades is exemplified in F. Scott Fitzgerald's novel *The Great Gatsby*, Cole Porter's songs, Noel Coward's plays, Cecil Beaton's photographs. People with status were civilized, cultured and immaculately dressed. They travelled, went on safari, took drugs and were involved in society scandals. Once again it wasn't a good thing to be poor (cf. the General Strike of 1926), and if you survived the crash of 1929 you were doing OK. If you survived all the Zeppelin crashes of the thirties you were doing even better.

In the roaring twenties it was best to be in Paris living La Vie Parisienne with Hemingway, Scott Fitzgerald et al. The place (and the currency) to avoid in both decades was Germany. A million marks could just about get you a cup of coffee if you were at the beginning of the restaurant queue – two million if you were at the end.

In the thirties the crowd to be in with in Britain was Edward and Mrs Simpson's. While in America it was movie people, specifically those who had successfully survived the transition to the talkies.

Clark Gable and Gary Cooper were the men to be seen with, Greta Garbo the woman. If you happened to be in France round about 1922, the surrealist movement was quite a trendy outfit to flirt with, provided you could get through to them on the lobster telephone. Finally, it was very trendy to fight for the republicans in the International Brigade in the Spanish Civil War. If you survived you could write many a macho tale of your exploits.

COVETED STATUS SYMBOLS: a cricket jumper, a cigarette holder, a mild headache.

Second World War

Even though the Navy was traditionally considered to be the 'Senior Service', being in the RAF during the Battle of Britain was the ultimate in glamour status in WW2. With a few enemy kills chalked up as swastikas on the jolly old fuselage, a battered old MG motor car with wire wheels, a dog called Skipper, and a couple of pals called Ginger and Pongo, young gels called Jean and Sally would find you simply irresistible. Correct elocution was an important aspect of status, and anyone who was anyone would be able to say 'Scramble' with complete authority.

If you were unlucky enough to be in the Army, a couple of pairs of nylons and a packet of Lucky Strikes were handy to have about your person when liberating the demoiselles of Europe. Surviving the whole conflict was, once again, the object of the exercise, though in a uniform, rather than a cushy civvy street number.

COVETED STATUS SYMBOLS: twelve square inches of colourful campaign braid above the left breast pocket of your uniform on VE day in 1945. A dusty, faded map with the location of hidden Nazi treasure.

The fifties

The fifties were the age of the aristocrats, the dire English B-movie and so-called 'modern living'. *Vogue* models came from the upper classes and photographers were all society gents – Anthony Armstrong-Jones (later Lord Snowdon), Norman Parkinson, and Cecil Beaton. English movies were thin imitations of the American product: racketeers called 'Boss', casinos, big cars and cigars and glamour girls; while the poorer end of the market were glamorized hanging around Soho coffee bars as leather jacketed hard-nuts and Teddy Boys.

The area to look for real status was in the home. Modern flats with nice futuristic-looking electric fires (NB: fireplaces carried no status at all in the fifties and were considered old-fashioned and so were removed in their thousands). Woodchip, veneer and mass-produced synthetic fabrics were all the rage. And if you had Formica? People would practically have multiple orgasms in your living room. To have status in the fifties, you had to be modern. You had to be the lead trumpet in a jazz band, you had to have a zoot suit, you had to dance like they did in *West Side Story*. Girls to have on the end of your arm were either Princess Margaret,

Doris Day or Diana Dors. The men were Sinatra, Gene Vincent and Herbert Lom.

COVETED STATUS SYMBOLS: a wall safe, Pepsodent toothpaste, a flick knife.

The sixties

In the sixties stereo or stereo records were the ultimate status symbol. No one had stereo except for parents, who rarely used the facility except for those odd times when Dad's birthday present arrived in the form of another volume of Herb Alpert's *Greatest Hits*. To buy stereo records even though you didn't have a stereo system to play them on was the ultimate in schoolkid status (apart from love bites): 'Sure I buy stereo records. I've also got a switchblade and a Ronson cigarette lighter. Also I know a girl who knows a girl who knows another girl who's actually on the Pill.'

Merseyside (The Beatles). Cambridge (The Pink Floyd, Clive James, Germaine Greer) and swinging London were the places to be. Stateside the place to be was New York, specifically at Andy Warhol's Factory, the person to be was a Warhol Superstar (though it was not necessary to go to all those openings of toilet seats like Andy did).

Back in Britain, Twiggy, Jean Shrimpton, Christine Keeler, Mandy Rice-Davies were the girls to be seen with. Mick Jagger, David Bailey, Terence Stamp, James Fox and a Beatle were the men. And anyone, my dear, who was anyone was working class (pop stars, photographers, property developers, models, actors, playwrights and fashion designers – i.e. everyone).

It's considered status today to have been around in this 'golden' decade of promiscuity, reform and radical politics, especially if you have some embarrassing photographs to show for it. Where people may have asked their fathers once what they did in the war, nowadays the question is, 'What did you do in the sixties, Dad, before you hung your Gibson acoustic up for good?'

COVETED STATUS SYMBOLS: a Mini Moke, a mock-Tudor mansion in Surrey, inflatable furniture, a sitar blessed by the Maharishi Yogi.

The seventies

Many believe the seventies to be one of the crassest cultural decades of the century. Nevertheless, the more pronounced the bell-bottom, the more dangerous the platforms, the wider the kipper tie, the more status you seemed to have, at least 'fashion'-wise. On the music scene it was considered a great sign of status if you saw Roxy Music's first tour, before they became well known, and Bruce Springsteen's first gigs in Britain in 1975, before he made it big. Advertising was the only profession to really excel itself creatively, and if you were at an agency known as Collett Dickenson and Pearce (employees included Alan Parker, Charles Saatchi, James Herbert, David Puttnam, Gray Jolliffe, Adrian Lyne, Ridley Scott, Hugh Hudson) you didn't need to look much further. Other institutions that carried status in this age of glitter and non-achievement were the *New Statesman* magazine, Pan Books, St Martin's School of Art and CBGBs Club in New York.

Punk was one of the few cultural achievements of the decade, an indication of how bad it was, and if you saw the Sex Pistols perform live before their demise, that was something to brag about. If you gave up being a punk before it became just another French fashion, you can claim original punk status.

COVETED STATUS SYMBOLS: bootleg Bob Dylan albums, a cheese-cloth skirt, an oil field.

Ten examples of status recently demised

1. The millionaire
Once it was fab to be a millionaire. Nowadays it's no longer very big deal to be one. With sky-high property prices, anyone who owns a house seems to be almost there. By the mid-1990s they say

you won't even be able to buy a one-bedroom toilet in Brixton for less than half a mill.

Now to be a billionaire, that's something else.

2. A Harrods' bag

Some people spend a couple of quid on a 20p pencil at Harrods, just to get that coveted green bag. A green Harrods' bag indicates that you've been to Harrods. Since everyone shops at Harrods nowadays, everyone must have a few of those jolly green bags gathering dust in that cupboard under the sink, so their exclusivity and status is minimal. In launderettes, a Harrods' bag might confer on you some kind of nebulous status as you bring your monthly load in; but if you're the type who looks for status in launderettes you're probably in need of psychiatric treatment anyway. Harrods' carrier bags simply last longer than other carrier bags, but that's not status, that's craftsmanship.

NB: Harrods the store holds on to its status as a place to shop by the skin of its teeth. Though a bit of a cliché it's still an excellent store. The department within that carries the most status is the Food Hall, not because all the stars shop there, but because the food is excellent.

3. *Spycatcher*

The living room today, toilet reading tomorrow, donated to the local fête the weekend after. Your dinner party host will boast that he picked it up in Rizzoli's bookstore on 57th Street, to the amazement of Daphne and Simon who thought that that was 'awfully illegal'. While we're on the subject, did anyone buy it illegally? Did you pay a fortune for a copy from a man in a raincoat on the M4? Did anyone buy it for 60p in a fête? Was it any good?

NB: it's important to bear in mind that status symbols must endure. For the price of a mere 16,000 *Spycatcher*s you could've bought a small Picasso etching. Now that would've been something to talk about.

4. CD (Corps Diplomatique)

Diplomatic immunity is not what it used to be since people protected by it started getting away with murder.

5. Caviar

Once the essential sustenance of the Martini Set, associated with Bond, bimbos and boudoirs. Now, since it is available at all leading corner shops, its coveted 'je ne sais quoi' has somewhat faded.

6. Fur coats

In the US and much of Europe fur coats are still big status with women. But in Britain, ever since the successful 'dumb animals' advertising campaign, they tend to look rather silly with spit on them.

7. Wall safes

So *de rigueur* in the fifties, wall safes appeared in every George Sanders and Herbert Lom B-movie, those 'Casino-acting-as-a-front-for-the-Organization' type movies, where the safe was found behind the painting of the Spanish tart behind the desk, where the combination was always the same – two to the left, one to the right, followed by fifteen seconds of frantic random twisting. Wall safes always carried some vital incriminating documents, some 'hot ice', some international currency and a plastic pistol which was invariably used to try and plug the hero in the final scene. Nowadays everyone uses a bank. But we can all foresee a time when wall safes might make a come-back. They're so kitsch.

8. Cigarette holders

These were big status symbols in the eras of Noel Coward and Tallulah Bankhead. Today they'd be considered both pretentious and dangerous.

9. An ex-directory telephone number

With the state of British Telecom you'll be glad of any phone calls you can get, so it's best to be in the phone book: 'You got a heavy breather? I was luckier. I got an insurance salesman.'

10. Suntans

Maybe not today. Maybe not tomorrow. But soon, and for the rest of your somewhat foreshortened lives.

SOME CATEGORIES OF STATUS

The status non-starter

He brings his Porsche into the conversation whenever he can. He says things like 'there is only one Porsche', presumably referring to whichever model his company bought for him. He is forever booking tables at Langan's Brasserie and forever pestering 'Cainey' to sign his menu – so he can convince the other sales reps at the office that he is mixing with 'heavy company'. He wears an incredibly expensive seventies 'Tommy Nutter' suit with exceptionally wide lapels, topped off with an even more expensive pair of grey shoes. His most prized possession is a snapshot of him and Ronnie Biggs (endearingly referred to as 'Biggsy') taken in Rio two summers ago in a nightclub. He is a hi-fi bore. His lifetime's ambition is to have a Lamborghini Countach.

Porto Banus on the Costa del Crime is the pot of gold at the end of the rainbow for him. His wife calls him 'Babe', and spends most of her time under the sunbed at the Sanctuary Health Club. Her idea of status is to name their children Wayne and Di.

The status misguided

He buys an E Type Jaguar Series 2 with a hardtop, instead of a Series 1 with a soft top. He tells the waiter to keep the change at McDonald's. She confuses *Budgie* with opera, and the Costa del Sol with the Côte d'Azur. They bought limited edition prints from Christie's ten years ago for £75 apiece. They're currently worth £76 apiece. They went to the opening night of Stringfellow's, Macclesfield where they met several members of the Tremeloes and Dave Dee, Dozy, Beaky, Mick and Titch. If he could live his life all over again he'd be a DJ, she an air stewardess.

The status beginner

His salary has just hit five figures (i.e. £10,500). She has just bought a sunlamp at the local auction. They recently met their first celebrity, Lance Percival, backstage at the local panto, and swiftly made their first inroad into the inside track by inviting him to their drinks party. They splash out on champagne and it isn't even Christmas. They know some freemasons who might be able to get them in. They drive a 1973 Yellow Lotus Eclat. He takes copies of *GQ* from the office and leaves them casually on the bathroom floor. She wears Janet Reger underwear under her tights.

He's desperate to date the boss's daughter who only agrees so she can spite her father. She doesn't mind being seen in the company of First Division footballers.

Last year, they visited New York, but they stayed in Queens rather than in Manhattan. Together they look like a TV building society ad couple.

The status slave

Both he and she are ardent opera buffs. Naturally they don't go for the music. They go to be seen. They are easy prey for photographers and paparazzi. They wear all the latest fashions, and allow their homes to be splashed across *House and Garden* and *Interiors*. They pronounce Joseph, the fashion shop, 'Jozeffff'. Their lives are a series of speedy TV channel changes. They follow the antics of 'The Tina Chow Set' in all the social pages. He is obsessed with Paul Smith attire, and finds every occasion to use his Mont Blanc Meisterstuck pen. She has a Bulthaup kitchen though she's never cooked in it. He says things like, 'it's time to go it alone,' and 'I've got the backing.' She clutches her Y.S.L. handbag and replies in a perfectly manicured voice, 'Fanty-astic.' Their whole lives are spent trying not to be in the same place for more than three days at a time. They've been everywhere, they've seen everything, but they've never had time to enjoy a thing.

Superior status

People with superior status do everything perfectly. Their lives are carefully structured around each and every manifestation of status expression and convention. And they adhere rigidly to the 'invisible' profile rather than the 'obvious', blatant forms of status. Since they are the subject of this book, and dealt with in detail, the only way to give a quick insight into their rarefied situation and how they came to arrive there is to observe them in some of their natural habitats and situations (see Top Status).

At an auction

You're at an auction and the auctioneer recognizes that slight changes in the colour of your irises implies a raised bid of five grand. The audience gasps in amazement as you outbid the Aga Khan, who shakes his head in despair.

In a bar

You order a round of drinks and you say, 'Put it on my tab, would you, Conrad/Quentin/Luigi.' He, with his usual wise-cracking good humour, replies, 'Yessir, certainly, sir. It'll be a pleasure, sir. Will that be all, sir?'

In a restaurant

You say, 'My usual table, please,' to the slightly over-fawning Maître d', and, as he summons legions of garçons to take your coat away, you add, 'Could you put a bottle of your very best on ice, I'm expecting company.' 'Mais certainement, monsieur,' he replies subserviently, as he backs away into the sweet-trolley.

In the casino

People overhear the pit-boss tell the croupier that Mr Bond's (no relation) credit is good here, as the beautiful young countess opposite finds herself unexpectedly charged with great sexual expectation. 'Hi, I'm Plenty,' she quips.

At the nightclub

You walk past Nell's in New York en route to the 711 corner store when suddenly the doorman, who has just turned away De Niro and party, begs you to come in, if only for a while, tattered dressing-gown and all, drinks on the house.

In your absence
In your absence, the social elite of the City are gathering to plan the party to end all parties, when someone is heard to say, 'But surely no party would be complete without Rick de Montfort?' Exeunt all but the man who suggested the party in the first place, who commits hari-kari in the jacuzzi.

As you gracefully fish out a cigarette from your coat pocket
A stampede ensues, as people tumble over each other to light it for you.

As deadlock arises in a prison riot
The head of the bad guys (who despite their badness have a bona fide grievance about conditions in the prison) shouts to the governor (who is surrounded by guards all sporting Winchester pumps), 'We'll only negotiate with Cyril Dodds. Otherwise we start throwing the bodies out.' Seconds later the governor is on the line begging you to come down to the prison to quell the riot.

Your reputation (good or bad) going before you
'I have heard many things about you, Cyril Dodds, but never in my wildest dreams did I imagine such a formidable adversary.'

The phone conversation with Eric Clapton or Mark Knopfler
Eric: Hello, Mrs Dodds, is Cyril in?
Mrs Dodds: Not at the moment. He's out visiting the poor and the sick in the community.
Eric: Well, this is Eric here. I wonder if you could ask him when he gets home whether he'll play on my new album?
Mrs Dodds: Oh, what a coincidence, Eric. Mark Knopfler's just been on the phone asking exactly the same question.

FROM THE CRADLE TO THE GRAVE AND BEYOND – STATUS BEGINS AT THE VERY BEGINNING

It's where you were conceived

Status won't even wait till you're born, if it can help it. From around the time you're a twinkle in your daddy's winkle, it's there, making plans for you. Because exactly where you were conceived could make all the difference. For most of us it's of no importance – between the sheets, in wedlock, the last Sunday of the month. But what if it were on a warm beach under the cherry moon on a Maldivian island? Your beloved mama and an exotic non-English-speaking eastern potentate, who later disappeared into the night never to be seen again. What if it were in the back of Ed Bankey's car in a moment of teenage lust? Or at a Hell's Angels' gang bang? What if you were conceived in a test tube? Which of these situations are you most likely to admit to *Time* magazine later on in life? OK, so you were conceived normally. What about your ancestors? Anyone to brag about?

Your ancestry

Everyone has a family tree, whether they know it or not. Everyone must therefore have someone worth having as an ancestor. Since we all have thousands of ancestors (your mother's great-grandmother's sister's great-uncle's bastard son's cousin's whore-mongering innkeeping grandmother, who slept with the Prince Regent's nephew, giving birth to a son who is currently sixtieth in line to the throne), the first rule is that a famous ancestor ought to have your surname, i.e. the surname of your father.

Secondly, since everyone is ultimately related to both royalty and God, it carries more status if your forebears were renowned for something more notorious or heinous, for example highway robbery, or for being a deviant or a revolutionary, someone like Wat Tyler, who at least made some media impact on the times they lived in, if only in the gruesome circumstances of their execution.

Which side did your ancestors fight on in the Wars of the Roses? Whose side were they on in the Civil War? These are questions that have often been asked by judges of status. In fact it doesn't really matter one way or the other, so long as your ancestors weren't the sort who sat on the fence, like those innkeepers in World War Two movies who had a photograph with Winston Churchill on one side and a picture of Adolf on the other. Some historical connection with the Russian Tsars always goes down well, as does a blood connection with famous artists, musicians and nineteenth-century courtesans or colonial femmes fatales – like Greta Scacchi in *Heat and Dust*, Greta Scacchi in *White Mischief*, Greta Scacchi in *White Lingerie*. In answer to the oft asked question, is it status to be linked to Ludwig II of Bavaria, the answer is categorically 'no'.

Where were you born?

Does where you were born affect your status in later life? Not especially if it's in a hospital or at home (unless, of course, it was in the next cot to Prince Harry or Prince William). But supposing it was in the back streets of Naples. Or in a field. Or on a hill surrounded by wolves. Or in a crossfire hurricane. Or in a traffic jam in a Hollywood movie. Supposing your parents were part of a tribe or sect where new-born babies were left out overnight to test whether they were a strong child, and you survived the ordeal. That would be a story to casually recall in the future, at your club. Apart from highly unusual circumstances, not many really dwell too much on the geography of their birth.

What was your upbringing like?

What happened to you when you were a child could have a very strong influence on your status later in life. Privileged upbringings don't necessarily carry more status than underprivileged ones, except perhaps at the time. The point is to capitalize on your upbringing, bad or good, in a positive way.

A tough upbringing and status

Starved and beaten. Your old man an alcoholic. Your old lady a tramp. The mean dustbin-lined streets, amid the pool rooms and flop houses, where you had to learn to survive or go under. Your switchblade often the only friend you had. The reform school. The foster parents who hid the fact that you were a love child. All this is the stuff of blockbuster novels and TV mini series. A tough, underprivileged upbringing can count heavily in your favour status-wise, so long as you become rich and famous later on.

Bryan Ferry has dined out on many a journalist's expense account describing his mining town origins. And we are no stranger to the many rock stars and artists who relish in revealing their hungry sojurns in basements just so they can later say that they suffered for their Art.

Clawing your way to the top from a disadvantaged position generally carries a lot of status. It is, after all, the American way. And providing you don't retain too many of your Eliza Doolittle characteristics, providing you remember to use a knife and fork at embassy dinners, and to say 'bathroom' instead of 'kazi', the romantic image will remain intact.

A privileged upbringing and status

Privileged upbringings carry status in later life, provided they too are capitalized on. Status observers look dimly on those children and youths who don't exploit these 'advantages' and make a hash of it in adulthood. Strangely, if you are successful later on, the practice is usually to gloss over your background with a wave of hand, or even treat it with slight scorn, rather than publicize it.

There has always been a fascination for those figures who, in the face of money, privilege and title, reject everything (apart from the odd Armani outfit) and go and join the Communist Party or some extreme left-wing organization dedicated to the over-throw of that which gave them a head start in the first place, for example Patty Hearst, the Baader-Meinhofs, Blunt, Burgess, Maclean et al. This is one classic example of inverted status.

THE CHRISTENING: Following your painless, hygienic birth, your first status landmark is usually six weeks later on the day of your christening. Status on this day will usually be determined by who attended, your godparents, and your gifts.

WHO ATTENDED: A quick look at the faded guest list in the family photo album may reveal the likes of Lady Di, Peter Cook (an old drinking chum of your father's) and several members of U2. Everyone agreed at the time that it was a great bash for a christening, and even if they didn't totally remember you in later life, the photos in the social pages of the society magazines of the day will certainly remind them.

GODPARENTS: The more godparents the better. More than the famous celebrity guests, godparents are the ones that are supposed to help you later on in life. If one of them happens to be called Corleone, well and good.

GIFTS: A silver cup, silver booties, a couple of quid to kick off your Coutts account – these will probably be the first of many status symbols you have in your life. A silver spoon start is no bad thing.

A childhood of nannies and servants and cooks called 'Cook' is further evidence of privileged upbringing. Nannies are better than au pairs in terms of status, though au pairs still count for something. Later on in life, you are as likely to take time off from your busy City job and visit your old nanny as you are your mater and pater.

During the course of your privileged childhood, trips to Hamleys are frequent, and the presents just get better and better. Your clothes are always expensive (Oilily, Portofino, Patrizia Wigan, La Cigogna, Burberry and Y.S.L.) your shoes are measured Clarkes and Start-Rites and the expression 'hand-me-down' is unheard of, except in relation to the breakfast cereal on the top shelf in the kitchen, for example, 'Cook, will you please hand me down the Shreddies from the top shelf.'

Piano lessons, tennis lessons, ballet lessons, riding lessons (yes, of course you've got your own pony) and swimming lessons are all foisted on the status brat to give them every possible future advantage. It should be remembered that the more status you enjoy as a child, the more status will your parents enjoy among their friends. Parents with status children just live for the day when another mum or dad says just within earshot: 'That child has just composed a piano concerto at the age of six? God, he must have talented parents!'

Childhood status symbols

0–1: Peaudouce nappies, a porcelain potty, a silk 'wet' blanket.

1–3: Your first books are first edition Beatrix Potters and Winnie the Poohs.

3–5 Your teddy bears are old, priceless and antique, just like the one that nice boy Sebastian Flyte had in *Brideshead Revisited* on TV.

7–11 Your daddy's priceless lead soldiers and electric train set are yours on your ninth birthday. You move on to hardback Tintin (never paperback, too vulgar). You already own the complete collection of *Thomas the Tank Engine* videos. Your dolls and dolls' house were about to be donated to the V&A museum and then you were born. Needless to say they're priceless. Other status books by the bedside include first edition Tolkien, *The Hobbit* and *Lord of the Rings*. A BMX bike is already awaiting. And lastly, since it's never too early to start networking with other silver spoon kids, parties are many and raucous. For maximum future influence these are attended by kids of all nationalities dressed in Benetton clothing.

Status is your education

From the nursery to university and beyond

Where you went to school, what you learnt, who you went to school with; all these are very important aspects that will affect your status in later life. Of course it's important to pass exams to move up the educational ladder. But swotting is only one aspect of educational status. For example, going to school and befriending a junior royal or the daughter of a List 'A' celebrity, even though you consistently fail exams, is far more significant to the status of your education than passing O Level woodwork.

Where once private tutors were considered the ultimate in educational status, because you had total individual attention and you didn't catch head lice from the other kids, nowadays they are considered a bit wet and, unless coupled with an outside education, they hardly prepare you for the dog-eat-dog world outside.

When it comes to the choice of a more traditional or modern education there's no competition if you're out to maximize your, or your sibling's status – traditional every time and preferably private. The names of your schools – 'We were at Eton together' – the names of your professors – 'Old Jossers a Nobel Prize winner? Good grief, he was my tutor at Oxford' – the names of your school chums – 'The new Home Secretary? I was at school with him' – these future avenues of status and influence all start at the 'right' school.

In England the 'right' schools are essentially 'vair' British. They are reminiscent of the schools portrayed in *If* and *Another Country* rather than *St Trinian's*. School life was tough and even if corporal punishment was a thing of the past, there was nothing to stop other kids trying to flush you down the bog if you were a swot. If the hierarchy of the 'gods' of *Another Country* no longer exists, being a prefect, head of house or captain of the school still enables you to exert a fair amount of power and influence at an early age. Between Latin lessons and the rugby field, you learn such essentials as team spirit, not to suck up to teachers, not to sneak, not to swot, not to cry, and basic good old-fashioned contempt for everyone outside 'the school'. You rub shoulders and share showers with boys and girls who will go on to take up jobs and positions running the world. And as an Old Boy or Old Girl it's obviously your job to help them.

At the end of the day the benefits of education status-wise are derived from mixing with an educated elite – an old boy network that you will keep in with after the school gates have long shut behind you. The outcome of many a job interview, the invitation to many an essential party, the successful application to many a club or board membership may well depend on your status. And despite the best qualifications in the world it could well go against you if you are not fondly remembered from schooldays: 'Yes, I know Stinker Stonehouse would be ideal to run our Hong Kong office, but he sneaked on Jism Major in a school chemistry test, so there's no way he's getting my vote.'

As time goes on, however, they become less important, as your subsequent achievements outshine your origins. Yet there remains an element of snob status if you did attend the 'right' schools and universities. (If you went to a comprehensive school you don't tend to shout it from the rooftops.)

Naturally school fees for such an early boost to your status are going to be crippling. But for parents and children alike these are looked on as a sound investment.

Schoolboy/schoolgirl status

In the film *If* it was status to be up against the system, blow up the school and kill everyone in it (a bit extreme). In *Ferris Bueller's Day Off* status involved playing truant in a borrowed Ferrari. In *Gregory's Girl* in was a question of feminine one-upmanship where the heroine was a soccer-mad girl who succeeded in getting a place in the school team because she was a more skilled player than any of the boys. In *Risky Business* Tom Cruise runs an upmarket call-girl service for his chums and ends up securing a place in college as a result. In *Tom Brown's Schooldays* status was taking care of the school bully. Nothing's really changed, then.

- Winning silver cups and having your name (plenty of initials and a long surname) engraved on them (preferably three years in a row).

- Beating shit out of the school bully, after he mistakenly thought you were 'a soft touch' (boys). Accidentally dropping concentrated sulphuric acid on the female school bully's lap in chemistry lesson (girls).

- Speaking French better than the French teacher. 'Monsieur, vous avez fait un faux pas.'

- Calculating a sum mentally faster than Watson Major who uses a pocket calculator.

- Making an atomic bomb in chemistry.

- Being called a 'child prodigy', but still being able to have a good time with your chums.

- Hacking Prince Philip's mailbox (again) on the school computer.

- Girls: looking older than they are.

- Boys: being able to grow some downy stubble above your upper lip that doesn't resemble a cluster of blackheads.

- Girls: being among the first to wear a brassiere in the class.

- Boys: the first to beat off faster than Undermanager senior after lights out.

- Scoring the winning try (rugby), goal (hockey) against your school's biggest rival, and being mobbed afterwards by pitch-invading hoards.

- Fooling everyone that the birthmark on your neck is actually a love bite.

- Scoring a goal at St Andrew's Day wall-game at Eton.

- Spending your days in a wistful, lackadaisical 'all life is meaningless' pose while indulging in some 'heavy' revolutionary reading, for example Marx, Engels, Darwin, the more sensitive side of Vlad the Impaler, advanced Scargill, Machiavelli's *The Prince*, *Things Thai Girls Like*, Proust, Jean-Paul Sartre, *The Essence of Nihilism*.

- Successfully blackmailing your form teacher to give you a glowing end of term report. 'Rupert has shown consummate skill in always being in the right place at the right time. The Special Branch could indeed use a fellow like him.'

- Being expelled on the grounds that 'school has nothing more it can teach you.' (NB: expulsion, despite its anarchic overtones, doesn't automatically mean schoolchild status. Each case must be judged on its merits.)

Some public schools that carry status
BOYS
Ampleforth College, Yorkshire
Charterhouse, Surrey (Genesis pop group went there)
Eton College, Berkshire
Fettes College, Edinburgh
Gordonstoun (the royal princes went here)
Harrow School, Middlesex (Andrew Nitch-Smith went here)
Marlborough College, Wiltshire
Milton Abbey School, Dorset
Winchester College, Hampshire
Wellington College, Berkshire
Stowe School, Buckinghamshire

GRAMMAR SCHOOLS THAT CARRY STATUS: Wimbledon College Grammar, Wimbledon (the author went there).

GIRLS
Benenden, Kent
Roedean, Sussex
North Foreland Lodge, Hampshire
Heathfield, Berkshire
Downe House, Berkshire
Cranbourne Chase, Wiltshire
St Mary's – Berks, Wilts and Oxon
Sherborne School, Dorset
Stonar School, Wiltshire
Tudor Hall School, Oxfordshire
West Heath, Kent
Wycombe Abbey, Buckinghamshire

Finishing Schools
A little old-fashioned nowadays. Especially as the idea tra-ditionally implied completing the young lady's education so that

she could catch the 'right' man and subsequently keep him with the magnificence of her understanding of economics, culinary skills and amazing dress sense. Finishing schools smack a little of Japanese geisha culture, where the idea is to teach a range of social graces for the prime purpose of being suitable mates to the highest in the land and their friends. If you must go to finishing school, forget Lucie Clayton and go abroad. At least in Switzerland you may get some skiing in.

Universities

Basically there is just a choice of three. Cambridge, Oxford and Liverpool. (Why Liverpool? Because the author went there.)

STATUS CAMBRIDGE COLLEGES: Trinity is the richest and most powerful, the largest landowner in the country after the Crown and the Church. Provider of many a Nobel Prize winner (once, more than the whole of France) despite having a reputation for being academically middling.

The status rule is, the more traditional and bigger, the more status (St John's, Magdalene, Jesus). If you consider booze and sports to be signs of status go to Pembroke. Essentially it's best to have a college in town, in a formal setting and with rooms in traditional hall buildings (as in *Brideshead Revisited*). Smaller colleges tend to be more academic (Clare, Trinity Hall, Corpus, Selwyn) while overall, Cambridge is science-orientated to Oxford's arts. The newer colleges (Robinson, Churchill) set ridiculously high entrance and academic standards to attract attention. Depending on your own particular definition of status, Peterhouse is or isn't, depending on whether you're a National Front supporter and anti-homosexual, or not.

STATUS OXFORD COLLEGES: All Souls: the highest form of intellectual status at Oxford is to become a Fellow of All Souls. Leo Amery once referred to All Souls as a 'world-wide secret society pledged to see that its members are ensconced in all the key positions of public life'.

Balliol is essentially socialist, and provider of lots of Prime Ministers and Cabinet Ministers. Christ Church is the richest and most political college, home of the beagle pack. It has a great lawn for weddings. Trinity: is old and traditional, with a croquet lawn.

THE OXFORD UNION: The late eighties Oxford Union is a hot one politically, artistically and personality-wise. To be president is high status indeed, and this will guarantee you even more status after you've completed your studies.

OXFORD AND CAMBRIDGE STUDENT STATUS ACTIVITIES: Where once it was a sign of student status to adopt a foible, a pose, an eccentric way of dressing, where once it may have been considered status to investigate the mysteries of homosexual practice even if you felt 100 per cent heterosexual; or to ascend the vines and walls of girls' colleges for some rumpy pumpy with some delicate creature without getting caught, nowadays many of these activities are considered passé since they are no longer that shocking. As with everything in life, it's becoming harder and harder to be original, to stand out. (NB: it's not even possible to paint the pillar box outside Clare College since the Post Office finally removed the offending article.)

The trick of student status is to poke your finger in the eye of tradition cleverly rather than heavy-handedly, for example freeing the prisoner in the Amnesty International cage outside King's simply by setting fire to it, putting an articulated lorry on Senate House, etc.

MAY BALLS AND BUMPS

BALLS, CAMBRIDGE: The best and most expensive (£150 a double ticket) is probably Magdalene, which tends to be the only white tie affair (harder to gatecrash), followed by Queens' and Trinity Ball. Gatecrashing them is a form of status simply because the better ones are extremely difficult to get into: greased college roofs, security guards on land and in kayaks on the river, make gatecrashing a challenge worthy of James Bond: 'He floated face down in a drifting punt, with only a cold bottle of Bollinger '63 for company. His one thought was of rescuing her from the crashing boredom of her odious male escort. With SMERSH guards watching every entrance, his task looked impossible.'

BALLS, OXFORD: Christ Church. The biggest and best.

BUMPS: To beat all comers, especially any European competitors. Rowing is the thing to be taken seriously at Oxford and Cambridge. And if you represent the university at the annual Boat Race you've entered the top status class (at least that's what the outside world thinks – students aren't that bothered so long as it's an excuse for a piss-up).

NB: One of the Cambridge events of the year is to be entertained at home by the Pieronis at their Albert Street residence.

Academia

At the end of the day, it helps to have a few academic qualifications; a few doctorates or a double starred first at Cambridge, or a congratulated first at Oxford, to show for your trouble. The subject is important. Traditional degrees like classics, history and law with obscure dissertations, are favoured over estate management or something really useful like popular cybernetics.

To be a Rhodes scholar (Kris Kristofferson, etc.) from the US is also status.

In the US there is a much clearer definition of the colleges which excel in a particular field of learning. It's not enough to say that you wish to go to Harvard or Yale in the States, in the same way you might say you want to go to Oxford or Cambridge in Britain simply because they carry greater overall clout. In the US you first decide on your preferred course of study, and then see which college offers the best course of tuition in that field.

Intellectual status

Intellectual status doesn't really have anything to do with university education. Instead it draws its status influence more from Europe, where, for better or worse, there was always some poseur of an intellectual giving everyone grief about the meaningless of existence, while sucking on an empty pipe and surreptitiously grabbing your girlfriend's (or boyfriend's) ass. Either that, or some monstrously clever being in a thin and sickly frame whom everyone regarded as 'the most brilliant mind of his generation' and who died of academic exhaustion aged twenty-two having just completed 'a theory'. France, in particular, was a breeding ground for intellectuals, writers like Sartre and Camus, Surrealists like André Breton and Renoir, while in Britain one is reminded of the likes of W. H. Auden, Stephen Spender, Christopher Isherwood and Aldous Huxley.

A thoroughly good time to have been an intellectual was in the nineteenth century, and in this century in the twenties. A bad time was under dictators (Mao, Hitler, Stalin) who weren't intellectual at all. In these times it carried a lot of status to be exceptionally thick (mentally as well as physically) and mindlessly hearty.

In the eighties most of the East European bloc countries have an intellectual elite. In Western Europe, obsession with money and material things means they've all but disappeared. Bernard Levin and George Steiner are among the few voices in the British wilderness.

IQ RATING: An extremely high one gives great status to its owner, so long as he or she doesn't let it get in the way of having a good time. If someone can be heard to say about yourself or a friend, 'She may look like a bimbo with that body, but she's actually got an IQ of 145', you ought to be laughing. Normal Intelligence Quotients are between 85 and 115. Only 1 per cent of people in the US have an IQ of 140 or over, so it's easy to gauge where your status lies.

NB: it has been estimated that John Stuart Mill (English writer and economist) had an IQ of 190, the German poet Goethe 185, Thomas Chatterton, poet, and Voltaire, the French writer, both 170. When you consider the IQ rating of the average football hooligan is only 23, that's not bad going.

What's in a name?

Names carry status. Doors are more likely to open, restaurants are more likely to take an unsolicited booking, people are more likely to say, 'I know who you mean,' (when they haven't got a clue), if your name is Andrew or Marion Nitch-Smith (income unknown) as opposed to Mick and Sadie Douchebag (income unknown).

It's a sad fact of life, but names can, and do, add to your status. That's why so many people change them (for everyone to later drop them). Goodbye, Norma Jean, Harry Webb, Archibald Leach, Reg Dwight, Richard Starkey, Alfred von Konigsberg. Hello, Marilyn Monroe, Cliff Richard, Cary Grant, Elton John, Ringo Starr, Woody Allen.

Could John Wayne really have cut it as Hollywood's tough guy all those years if he'd kept Marion Morrison as his name? And Issur Danielovitch Demsky, latterly Kirk Douglas? One doubts it very much.

Hollywood apart, names are very important to us mere mortals as an indicator of status. It's a quirk of fate that makes the name Philip Kerr totally acceptable, but Wayne Kerr a figure of schoolboy amusement.

Christian names are as important as surnames with regard to status. For example, Christian itself is a name that conjures up a sensitive, Gallic, Gitane-smoking, château-bound, handsome aristocrat. Whereas 'Del' unfortunately doesn't.

FOOTBALLER FORENAMES SHOULD BE AVOIDED if you expect your child to have an equal chance in the status stakes of the future. Avoid therefore names like Bobby, Ron, Frank, Les, Terry and Dave. Also movie star names should be avoided for anyone except real movie stars – so forget it, all you Troys, Clarks, Rocks, Kims, Tabs and Clints. Sixties psychedelic names such as Petuli, Zowie, Jet, Harmony, Saffron and Jade should consider taking another kind of trip. And below-stairs names such as Dora, Mollie and Elsie place their owners squarely at one end of the social scale. Equally, upper class names like Torquil, Peregrine, Perdita, Persephone, Lancelot and Lorelei convey on their owners little else but 'I'm a plonker' status. And lastly, should you consider the ultimate status profession to be that of cleaning woman, get yourself a jewel of a name like Pearl, Ruby or Amber.

SURNAMES ARE AS IMPORTANT AS FORENAMES WITH REGARD TO STATUS especially if they are genuinely double-barrelled. Dropping one of the barrels, as in Tony Benn for Anthony Wedgwood-Benn, doesn't affect the status one bit, it actually enhances it. On the other hand, if one of the barrels is fabricated, i.e. by surreptitiously adding her surname to his following marriage, then the alarm bells may indeed ring. 'Ladies and Gentlemen, a warm welcome for Trevor and Dagmar Wright-Pratt.'

Another trend for people trying to increase their status through name changing is to have an exceptionally long name with the odd 'de la' or 'Saint' something-or-other thrown in, for example, Justin de Villeneuve (Twiggy's ex-manager), and Terence Trent D'Arby. The rule here is that provided it's not too over the top, you might just get away with it. But beware of overdoing it, all you Jacques Yves Guy de Maupassant de St Honoré le très Bon-Smiths.

NICKNAMES RARELY ADD STATUS: With the exception possibly of 'The Boss', 'The Duke' (John Wayne) and 'Bird' (Charlie Parker). The nickname 'Yozzer' never enhanced anyone's status.

SILLY NAMES ARE JUST SILLY: Sting. Prince. Bono. Fish. Kipper.

SHORTENED OR MISSPELT FORENAMES are just pretentious: Marc with a C. Nic with a C. Jon without an H.

REPEATED NAMES, such as Robbie Robertson (former member of The Band), Humbert Humbert (Lolita's 'father'), Horst P. Horst (fashion photographer) have a quirky status ring about them.

Guinness, Sainsbury, Carnegie, Ford, Windsor, and Westminster are all handy handles to have somewhere in your name. But the ultimate name of all in terms of status is the one that's on everyone's lips.

Status is where you live and what you live in

You live in a fancy apartment off the Boulevard St Michel, where you keep your Rolling Stones records and a friend of Sacha Distel's? Maybe not, but where you live often says more about you than the size of your feet. Totally international or totally

parochial? Town or country? Skye's the limit? It doesn't necessarily matter. Where you live and what you live in (or out of, in
the case of a suitcase) is a major status manifestation. It's also a
complicated one, since it depends on whose rules you follow.

Some international city addresses that give instant status

London: Belgravia and Knightsbridge
New York: The Upper East Side
Los Angeles: Holmby Hills and Bel Air
Paris: septième et huitième arrondissements
Sydney: Point Piper
Hong Kong: The Peak
Tokyo: Chiyoda
Dallas: Southfork

You wouldn't be doing wrong by living in any of these places.
They're all very exclusive and expensive. But they're also obvious
and they do sound a little as if you bought that old 'the estate
agent told me I ought to live somewhere expensive to indicate I'm
loaded' ploy. It's not enough to keep up with the Rothschilds to
ensure status. You've got to stay ahead of them and that means
you've got to be different. Not just one of the crowd. Look where
keeping up with them got Sherman McCoy, Tom Wolfe's millionaire hero in *The Bonfire of the Vanities* – a Park Avenue albatross
that he couldn't afford to keep up. Not convinced? Then consider
the following conversation overheard in a trendy cocktail bar
recently between two men and a woman:

FIRST MAN: I live in Belgravia. I shop in Knightsbridge. My private
art collection is housed in the septième arrondissement of Paris.
My antique jacuzzi collection is in an ex-movie star's home in LA.
WOMAN: Yawn!
SECOND MAN: I live in a low dive in New Malden. Cyril Dodds
hangs out there when he's in town.
WOMAN: You interest me strangely!

*   *   *

The point is that it may carry more status to live somewhere exciting, undiscovered or different before the rest of the world catches on. New Malden isn't everyone's cup of Java, I grant you, but Peter Bernard moved there in 1987 so it's only a matter of time before the floodgates are opened to this charming little Surrey backwater.

NB: unusual addresses, addresses that don't follow the crowd, particularly if in some exotic location, usually carry high status.

THE ALTERNATIVE STATUS ADDRESS LIST
The sole resident or family on an obscure windswept island in the Hebrides. C/o Penguin's Point, The Ice Cap, Antarctica

- The Farmhouse, Provence (three months of the year only)
- The hunter and writer's shack, the middle of Colorado
- The mountain top villa, Tuscany (preferably out of season)
- With the Aborigines in the Australian outback (no fixed address)
- C/o the Indians, the rainforest, up the Amazon
- Just anchored off the Great Barrier Reef, Australia
- Room 23, The Crumbling Old Colonial Hotel, Shanghai
- The apartment at the top of the Chrysler Building in New York (see the Ridley Scott film *Someone to Watch Over Me*)

OTHER STATUS HABITATIONS TO LIVE IN
- The lap of luxury
- A penthouse
- The Old Rectory
- The Old Vicarage
- A lighthouse (remember the hideaway of the hero in *Diva*)
- An old converted church
- A cute little cottage with a cute little pastel moss-shaded roof, with a cute little garden, in which stands a cute ancient weather vane on a cute well-trimmed lawn rounded off with a cute little gate that's being sold for a cute 200 grand
- A crumbling castle with battlements and a friendly ghost
- A windmill with an interior worthy of a Knightsbridge town house
- An old mill house in complete working order, with a whizzo

stretch of unpolluted river and no access for riff-raff trespassers of the National Trust-rambler type.

BLOCKS OF FLATS: Even living in a block of flats can carry status, so long as the particular block of flats happens to be the Albany off Piccadilly, or the Dakota Building on Central Park West, New York.

STATUS SURROUNDINGS TO GO WITH YOUR HOME

A moat
A minefield
Some acres
A lodge by the front gate for an old family retainer
A driveway at least half a mile long
A real forest, rather than one of those phony tax-dodge types
An orchard
A maze
A trout stream
Stables
An indoor 'real tennis' court
An indoor swimming pool (at least in England)
A moor
An enormous service lift that goes right up to your studio apartment so you can ride your Harley Davidson straight into the living room

HABITATIONS NOT TO LIVE IN

The gutter
A sixties high rise
A ghetto
A project
A shack
A squat
A basement
A Salvation Army hostel
A houseboat
A fantasy

TOP STATUS LIVING

Your own private island – like Marlon Brando, Paul McCartney, and Ian Anderson of Jethro Tull

Your own mountain – like Robert Redford's Sundance in Utah

A palace or palazzo – like royalty, fashion designers and trade union leaders

A château – haunts of rich French people and rich foreigners

No permanent fixed address – you own so many properties that it's necessary to live two months here, three months there

LIVING IN THE COUNTRY, COMMUTING INTO TOWN: This is an indication of status, especially if it's from the right part of the country to the right part of town. Commuting from Milton Keynes to your job in Stoke Newington unfortunately doesn't count.

THE RIGHT SIDE OF TOWN AND COUNTRY: Just when you thought you'd scored the right living location, as the Harrods' removal lorry disappears over the horizon, you suddenly discover that, just as it's necessary to sit at the right table in the right restaurant to fully ensure status, there's a wrong and a right part of the right living location. You may as well not have a houseboat in Kashmir if it's not on the Srinagar side of the lake. And there are definitely two sides to Eaton Square. Mayfair may be the most expensive property on the Monopoly board but it's too full of shops and flashy foreigners to remain in the uppermost bracket. Since there are two sides to most upmarket addresses, extreme vigilance is called for if you are to retain top status.

THE RIGHT COUNTIES

Gloucestershire – especially around Tetbury and Cirencester. Prince Charles spends his weekends here

Hampshire – The Wallops, on the River Test, not Southampton way

Dorset – Cerne Abbas way, rather than east of Blandford

Cornwall – secluded parts of the north and south coast, Bodmin Moor, at least thirty miles from Newquay at any one time

Yorkshire – the north part

Norfolk – up and coming

IS DOCKLANDS STATUS? It's too early to tell. Docklands is still a long way from being completed and in this respect very dependent on economic factors and the health of the City. When the squeeze is on, Docklands' profile is less pronounced. Docklands' status is less to do with bricks and mortar anyway, more to do with ready-made lifestyles, high in space and privacy but low on community, which is reflected in the trendy image of the well-heeled yuppie.

So long as the image remains popular and highly prized, however, Docklands as an address will convey status. Prince Charles probably reduced the status (and value) of some dwellings when he rubbished their architecture on TV, but generally prices remain stable.

NB: Docklands has six subdivisions. The three prime areas are Wapping, Limehouse and the South Bank in that order. They offer reasonable communication with the City, impossible parking and a stable investment. Division Two is the Surrey Docks, the Isle of Dogs (site of the ambitious Canary Wharf Scheme) and Royal Docks (furthest away from the City).

ROOMS WITH A WATERY VIEW: The London property market (like many places) has discovered that the sheer undiluted pleasure of welcoming the day with a sight of the river has surpassed the cachet of fronting the park. Naturally, not any old stretch of water counts. But, with the exception of Vauxhall, most are worthy of consideration.

LIVING IN THE SUBURBS: Living in the suburbs doesn't convey any status in London. But in many countries in Europe and America it may do. It certainly does in Paris (Le Vesinet, St Cloud, Neuilly).

CITIES ON THE UP: Glasgow, Toronto, Vancouver, Shanghai, Leningrad, Havana, Prague, Chicago, Antwerp.

CITIES ON THE DOWN: Barcelona (over-exposure), New York (too overrated, too expensive, too dirty, too much of a drug problem), Rio, Milan.

STATUS ARCHITECTURE: Specifically Wren, Lutyens, Blunden and Shadbolt in the UK. Generally Edwardian, Victorian, Georgian and anything prior conveys status. Avoid fifties and sixties like your life depended on it (the way some of the sixties stuff was built it probably does anyway).

TO BLUE PLAQUE OR NOT? 'Trotsky, when he was in London for a short period of his life, lived twenty-three doors and three streets from this address.' Nuff said. Blue plaques can convey status. And there again, not.

Interiors

Furnishing the home
Like clothes, the way you furnish your home says a lot about your status. The trick is to seem as if you haven't tried too hard, while conjuring up a rich sense of style, taste and breeding. The moment someone walks into your home, the interior should immediately convey to them the superlative way in which you conduct your life and where you're likely to be found in the pecking order.

Badly chosen interior furnishings could completely obscure your true elevated status. It's unlikely someone will conclude on experiencing your diabolical taste in interior furnishings, 'This guy has terrific status but when it comes to furniture he just happens to be a total asshole.' They are more likely to conclude that they were previously taken in by the thin veneer of your superficial status, but a look inside your home has quickly made them wise to your severe shortcomings. With status, people look at the whole package.

There are few rules regarding the status of your home's interior and furnishings. If it looks like something out of *Interiors* magazine, or *House and Garden* (i.e. a magazine that costs more than £5 a time) well and good. If it looks like a shrine to the more recent cultural aberrations of souvenir Spain or Boarding House Britain then alarm bells ring. But one rule is that the more money you have at your disposal to furnish your house, the greater the mistakes that can occur. Sometimes, after several gaffes, you have on your hands what is commonly known as a folly, and this can be bad news indeed.

A folly is very difficult to define. You just know one when you see one. If you vomit soon afterwards, you've seen one. If you resemble a manic Ralph Steadman cartoon character, or the character from the painting *The Scream* you may just have experienced one. A folly is when nothing blends and nothing gels. It's intended to be a monument to beauty but ends up looking like fruit-bat excrement.

A folly may combine the more unsavoury remnants of the Victorian era and Empire days to give the impression of a museum rather than a home, for example stuffed animals and animal rugs, medical jars containing large pieces of cheap tribal leftovers, heavy mahogany-framed mirrors, matt black ghoulish figurines. Or cheap sixties novelties may predominate – bean bags, goatskin rugs, inflatable furniture. Or, at the other end of the scale, it may be the most expensive collection of antique furniture ever assembled, but you can't find a seat that won't make you feel as if you've been sitting on an Indian fakir's nail bed. A folly could easily be a house full of reproduction antique furniture (see The status misguided), or a house full of second-hand furniture that actually looks fourth-hand. A folly, quite simply, is a folly.

Another rule is that pictures are the quickest clue to their owner's status. Good original paintings and drawings are an indicator of what the rest of the place is going to be like. Many people with status also like to have their pictures lying on the floor propped up against the walls, a kind of 'I spent thousands on this picture and many weeks finding it, but I haven't found the time or the place to hang it'. (If in doubt on the picture question, the best thing is not to have any at all. Just plain white walls. People will then assume that your likes and dislikes are so obscure that there isn't a picture in existence that could possibly match your rarefied tastes).

The same for furniture. If in doubt over what type of coffee table to have, stick with an old tea chest till you're sure. 'A tea chest for a coffee table! So minimalist! So witty!'

ALARM BELLS: Formica, pine furniture, round white paper lampshades, Constable and Turner framed 'prints', corduroy sofas, red or yellow satin curtains, brown satin sheets, track lighting, flocked wall paper, imitation coal fires, Roman-style baths and jacuzzis, TVs in the toilets, imitation brick paper, a bar built from 'Pirate-style' rum barrels, silver-plated anything, certificates of merit adorning the living room (rather than the lavatory), telephone directories in the bookshelves.

NB: If in doubt about the interior of your home get David Hicks in fast.

A status room – the library

First of all it is considered a sign of status to have a library. If you can afford the luxury of one then you must be doing OK. Peace and quiet reigns in the library, children are forbidden there, and when guests arrive at your house they are informed that you are to be found 'in the library'. They eventually find you in some hidden corner, volume in hand, lost in thought. As they approach with reverence, you look up and, slightly startled, quickly inform them that the clue to solving the unified theory of the universe lies in a rare limited edition of one of the more squalid works of the Marquis de Sade. (You hope they believe this obvious lie, as you slip the book into your jacket pocket for further reading at bedtime.)

Jay Gatsby had an impressive library, Scott Fitzgerald informs us, but he used it to give his audience the impression of a breeding that he did not really possess. For libraries are impressive as status symbols, and no status home should be without one. Naturally you don't have to have rare and valuable books like those in the labyrinthine monastery library in *The Name of the Rose*, but some kind of exclusive collection must be in evidence. The volume must not just be of quality, but also of the most impressive edition, for example the American *The Bonfire of the Vanities* not the British one. First and limited run editions should be signed by the author, the inscription preferably personal.

The books can be about anything, from innocently illustrated children's books on cuddly donkeys, to the more impossible positions of the *Kama Sutra*, cuddly donkeys optional. The more banned books you have the better (cf. the Vatican's hit list). And it goes without saying that all paperbacks are forbidden.

SOME FIRST EDITION AUTHORS THAT INDICATE A STATUS LIBRARY: Samuel Beckett, Tolstoy, James Joyce, D. H. Lawrence, Oscar Wilde, the first English translation of Proust, Edgar Allan Poe. The poets Chatterton, Keats, Yeats and T. S. Eliot, and the illustrated William Blake. Darwin's *The Origin of Species*, Arthur Rackham's *Peter Pan*. A signed Evelyn Waugh, the complete set of Aubrey Beardsley's *Yellow Book*, *The Road to Oxiana* by Robert Byron. Early Steinbeck, Hemingway, F. Scott Fitzgerald. Science books and books on chess are a particular indicator of status.

SOME BOOKS AND AUTHORS THAT DON'T: The complete works of Shakespeare, Gideon's Bible, Clive James's novels, Jackie Collins (even if they are in hardback and signed by Jackie herself). Jeffrey Archer novels. Helmut Newton books of nudes, the adventures of Angelique, biographies of Gladstone and Enoch Powell, John Fowles second reprints, Barbara Cartland and Georgette Heyer, remaindered books from Susan Reynolds. How-to-make-love-to-the-bloke-next-door-for-the-rest-of-your-life books.

The wine cellar

Like a library, having a proper wine cellar at all is a great indicator of status. That means one specially constructed of bricks (brick floor and brick bins where the wine is laid) rather than an old bomb shelter where you keep your twenty-seven half-empty cans of Duckhams motor oil and several jars of miscellaneous screws.

According to Hugh Johnson the 'right' way to organize the cellar might go as follows: white Burgundies and German Ausleses laid down for maturing; bottles in racks (red, white and champagne) where they can be easily removed without disturbing others. These are ready for drinking. Then two more bins of red wines laid down for maturing, labels uppermost. Bottom row: claret stored in original cases from the château. Magnums of red Burgundy and Bordeaux. Vintage port binned for long ageing. Red Burgundy newly bought and not yet laid down.

Apart from a permanently bleary-eyed host who speaks in an incomprehensible tongue, tell-tale signs of a decent wine cellar might be an array of modern and antique decanting implements, funnels, candles for examining colour and monitoring sediment, an old table, plenty of cobwebs and dust, and odd black darkened misshapen bottles without labels.

Knowing a lot about wine and being famed for having 'a palate' or 'a nose' for wine are both signs of civilized status. Being able to identify the wine, the year, the vineyard and the grape at a tasting, with other experts, is high status indeed. Being able to say, 'I think you're mistaken, old boy. I think you'll find that it's a '61 rather than a '66,' is the right kind of status wine-speak. If you wish to further familiarize yourself with the fine art of wine appreciation, there is a whole language that needs to be learnt. It's not enough to say, 'This is a fruity little number, and no mistake.'

The ideal wine cellar will have a good scattering of first class growths and good years going back at least to 1970 and preferably beyond. The odd case of Château Pétrus (any year) is a must (on average £120 per bottle), Château Lafite, Mouton Rothschild and Latour, Château Cantemerle and Montrose. Have champagne in whatever vintage you fancy, preferably in Nebuchadnezzar or Methuselah form, Louis Roederer Cristal, Taittinger Crémant Blanc de Blanc. Vintage port is essential, especially '77, '70, '63, and '45. Any sign of Sainsbury's port, or Moët et Chandon shampers rouses extreme suspicion. As for Pomagne . . .

Food status

To eat or not to eat?

There is the image of the man or woman who never eats, never has the time, is all fired up on black coffee, countless cigarettes and amphetamines to get them through their wild, workaholic day.

There is the image of the professional person who goes to all the best restaurants and dinner parties but who only toys with the food, Dallas-style (surrounded on all sides by tall stemmed glasses full of 'designah wadah' and Californian white wine), while preferring to talk business.

There is the image of the man or woman who never eats breakfast or lunch, the Dirty Harry type who only has time to take a bite out of his over-filled fatburger before he must foil a bank robbery with greasy Magnum.

These images suggest that food isn't really all that essential and that status goes with a lack of it. But everyone knows that we have to eat and that even though lunch is a waste of time, there is a large amount of status attached to restaurant culture, from the haute cuisine Michelin star-studded affairs, to the caff that does the best fry-up this side of the Channel Tunnel.

Eating out

To score maximum status for choice and venue of restaurant, it's not enough simply to be seen in the best eateries. Any true status observer will tell you that you've got to sit at the right table as well for maximum points. The only way to find out for sure which are the best tables in a particular restaurant at a particular time of day is to study the guides, study the floor plans (to get you away from the kitchen and 'rest rooms', away from the slavering, foul-mouthed, big-bibbed Mr Creosote types) and observe those in the know. Attaining this type of knowledge will take time and you may have to book your table weeks in advance, but imagine the eventual buzz when all those keen young impressionable things come over and ask you to sign their menu.

Fortunately, the sting has been taken out of the status of *nouvelle cuisine*, so you no longer have to starve for your gastronomic elevation. No longer need you choke on that piece of orange peel stuck down your throat, no longer need the chef throw up his hands as you insist on the granny food that is once again popular (not your own granny's food, mind, but the Roux Brothers' granny.)

SOME INTERNATIONAL RESTAURANTS (AND BARS) WITH STATUS

LONDON: The Connaught Hotel, the Dorchester Grill Room, Le Gavroche, La Tante Claire, Le Caprice, Langan's (so out it's in), Harry's Bar, Green's Champagne and Oyster Bar. For tea: the Ritz, the Dorchester, Claridge's, Brown's.

OUTSIDE LONDON: Waterside Inn (Berkshire), Le Manoir aux Quat' Saisons (Oxfordshire).

PARIS: Jamin (Robuchon), Lucas Carton, Taillevant, Le Bernardin, Brasserie Lipp, Le Voltaire, La Coupole, Maxim's, La Tour D'Argent, L'Espace Cardin, Dodin-Bouffant. Bars: Aux Deux Maggots, Café de Flore, Hemingway Bar.

OUTSIDE PARIS: Michel Guérard (Eugénie-les-Bains), L'Espérance (Burgundy), Troisgros (Roanne), L'Oasis (La Napoule).

ROME: Hostario Dell'Orso, El Toula. Bars: Harry's Bar, Rosati.

FLORENCE: Enoteca Pinchiorri, Coco Lezzone. Bar: Giacosa.

MILAN: Gualtiero Marchesi, Bice.

VENICE: Bars: Harry's Bar, Gritti Palace.

GERMANY: Die Aubergine (Munich).

BELGIUM: Comme Chez Soi (Brussels).

SWITZERLAND: Girardet (Lausanne).

JAPAN: Kiccho (Osaka).

AUSTRALIA: Berowra Waters Inn (near Sydney), Stephanie's (Melbourne).

HONG KONG: Fook Lam Moon.

SOME US RESTAURANTS AND BARS

NEW YORK: Le Bernardin, Four Seasons, Le Cirque, Arcadia, La Grenouille, Harry's Bar, Mortimer's, Lutece La Caravelle, Harry Cipriani, Russian Tea Room, Au Bar, 21 Club.

CHICAGO: Le Français.

LOS ANGELES: Spago, Chasen's, Morton's, Regency Club, Trumps, The Bistro, Le Dome.

BERKELEY: Chez Panisse.

NEW ORLEANS: K'Paul's Louisiana Kitchen.

Food and shopping

Food status began with caviar. But it quickly moved on (see Symbols that clash). Today, there are all kinds of small food status manifestations which, taken together, give you an edge over others who aren't necessarily aware of the existence of such subtleties. It may never have bothered you what colour or type of bread you eat, but it is a well-known fact that brown scores more points than white, sliced loaves fewer points than the baker's crusty loaves, and that 'whole grain' and 'wheatgerm' are fairly essential ingredients in the status mix. In a country where Mother's Pride white sliced is easily the most popular staff of life, bread can say a lot about your breeding.

Eggs too can provide an easy bit of one-upmanship. Putting the salmonella argument to one side for a minute, if you buy premium-priced Free Range Eggs, you are in fact saying you don't mind paying extra for that old-fashioned, fast-disappearing farm quality that's essential to nourish your finely tuned status frame (to say nothing of your stance on 'battery' hen farming). The same was true of polyunsaturated fats.

If you fry bacon, rather than grill it, the fact that you came from lowly surroundings is written all over your cholesterol-saturated frame. And an old-fashioned Aga speaks volumes compared with one of those new-fangled microwave oven contraptions.

The list on food status is limitless. You can't eat plain old cardboard cornflakes any more without the muesli brigade jumping down your throats. And who cares if processed cheese makes a much neater sandwich, it's just not on. Time was when food could be enjoyed.

For some people where you shop for your canapés and hors d'oeuvres is all-important to your status. For others, so long as you have already acquired your status symbols, shopping is just a bore and a chore.

Some don't see status coming in to it with supermarket shopping. Some, however, like to maintain their status by putting all the boring purchases at the bottom of the trolley (salt 'n' vinegar crisps, detergents, cheap economy twelve packs of loo-roll) while putting all the exotic stuff on top – Bath Olivers, caviar, pâté de foie gras, orange peppers, unsalted butter, diamond necklaces . . .

EATING IN: It's a sign of status to give the odd dinner party. To maximize status, to become known as an essential dinner party host, a few dinner party rules must be observed.

1. The guest list is more important than the cuisine.

2. The blend of guests and their table positions also needs to be inspired, for example Clint Eastwood sitting next to Patsy Kensit sitting next to the Pope sitting next to Joanna Lumley sitting next to Mr Gorbachev is OK. Sitting Samantha Fox next to Arnold Schwarzenegger next to the Duchess of Kent next to Dirty Den next to Barbara Cartland is not.

3. Either mix people all from one industry, for example, showbiz, publishing, British Rail, or be a little more tangential, mixing the rich and powerful with the poor but intellectual.

4. A good excuse to throw a dinner party is because so-and-so's in town, or so-and-so's leaving town, or so-and-so's passing through town, or so-and-so has never left town, not even been across the Channel as far as I know, but they're such excellent company.

TABLE MANNERS: Table manners, like manners generally, are a definite indication of status:

The correct use of knife and fork.
When it's acceptable to use fingers.
The fact that chopsticks are very lowly in China, but apparently not here.
The correct passing of the port.
When you can and cannot smoke.
Which wines with which foods and courses.
Breaking a bread roll with hands, rather than using a knife.
How to ask your hostess for Heinz tomato ketchup without upsetting her.
When to gulp wines and when to sip them.

* * *

All these are examples of eating etiquette connected with status. If you must break the 'table manners' rule, break them all. Go the whole John Belushi hog, rather than just make one small faux pas: 'Everyone's stopped eating. I think I should have used the even smaller spoon for the sorbet.' Your hosts are more likely to forgive your former hoggism – 'Such wildness. Such beast-like qualities. I suppose we must make allowances for brilliance' – rather than the latter minor impropriety – 'I see Cynthia's scraping the bottom of the barrel again.'

Status is where you've been and what you've seen

Been?

Everyone's been to the moon. The world is such a small place that very few places we hear people have travelled to impress us. News of friends just having returned from Hong Kong and China is received politely, with a stifled yawn and some condescending remark like, 'How nice, I was there in 1978. Shortly after they opened the border, actually.' World travel doesn't amaze people any more. Everyone we know is either one step ahead of us, or one step behind. But we're all getting there. Nowadays, the only areas of the world that still offer status to the visitor or traveller are ones that remain largely unexplored, for example parts of Alaska, the Amazon Basin, Antarctica, The Arctic, Greenland, the Guiana Highlands in Venezuela (setting of Conan Doyle's *The Lost World* and W. H. Hudson's *Green Mansions*), Micronesia, (the Marianas, Marshall, Caroline and Gilbert Islands group, east of the Philippines), New Guinea and Rub' al Khali ('the Empty Place' – the most arid part of the Arabian desert). These are all the sort of places you'd expect to bump into a pith-helmeted David Attenborough accompanied by a diehard core of hardened bearded BBC cameramen. Apart from some of the more unexplored territories, there are odd countries that are forbidden, or can be visited for a limited period only (like Burma, parts of China and Asia), and some which are so exclusive, so difficult to gain access to that only the rich, adventurous and crazy can get there, for example the Maldives (near Sri Lanka, over 1,000 lush coral islands which are totally uninhabited), the outer Seychelles,

Lake Pedar in Tasmania, St Barthelmy, the Norfolk Islands, and the Galapagos Islands ('Isn't that Jacques Cousteau over there?')

Travellers who pride themselves on finding untried and untested areas in the world, particularly if they write about it afterwards, are accorded due status, especially if they travel alone and in dangerous territory. The late Bruce Chatwin's exploits in Patagonia, the Australian outback and West Africa are all reflected vividly in his books. Even Chatwin's tragically early death, reputedly for having consumed a thousand-year-old egg, was perhaps a better way to go than having a cardiac arrest in front of the TV. Paul Theroux is another status traveller/writer (*The Mosquito Coast, The Great Railway Bazaar*) who's been places. Not to mention Wilfred Thesiger and the queen of all travellers, Freya Stark.

OTHER PLACES TO HAVE BEEN THAT OFFER STATUS: To hell and back.

Seen?

Have you seen the following? Two minutes' dinner party silence if you have: the Pyramids, the Great Wall of China, the Yeti, the Loch Ness Monster, Ayers Rock, Angel Falls, Venezuela, the Temple of Abu Simbel, Halley's Comet, St Elmo's fire, moonbeams on the shores of Orion, the Easter Island Statues, a ghost, the Live Aid concert, a blue whale, a Sumatran or Javan rhinoceros, Syd Barrett (founder member of Pink Floyd), the Easter Bunny, Father Christmas.

Some places you may find status
Who's Who (a book of 'people who matter')
Who's Really Who (a book of 'people who really matter')
Burke's Peerage (aristos who matter, and those who don't)
Debrett's (similar to the above)
The Times' 100 Best Companies
'A life in the day of' (*Sunday Times* regular feature)
'A room of my own' (*Observer* magazine regular feature)
Jennifer's Diary (*Harper's and Queen* gossip column)
Granta (upmarket literary magazine)
Private Eye (satirical mag)

The Times obituary column
Vanity Fair (US style mag)

Some places where you won't find status

The Nigel Dempster and William Hickey columns (English tabloid
    gossip columns)

The *Sun*, the *Star*, the *News of the World* (though inverted
    snobbery status may reverse this)

The front cover of a magazine (there are so many magazines
    nowadays in circulation that everyone's been on at least one)

Terry Wogan

Any TV programme hosted by Noel Edmonds

Backstage

In most nightclubs

The office of Vice President

Behind the wheel of a Lamborghini Countach

In Paddington or Shepherd Market (nudge nudge, know what I
    mean?)

Stringfellow's

On Capital Radio

Cynthia Payne's tea parties

Status is whose party you get invited to

Or whose yacht, or dinner.

Invitations generally are a great indicator of status. Tell-tale
signs may be people shuffling through the gold-embossed invites
on stiff cards on your mantelpiece (several old Truman Capote
invites have been dusted off and left out especially for this
purpose) as they mutter enviously to themselves: 'Patsy Kensit,
Princess Diana and Darryl Hannah joint birthday celebration . . .
Sonya Shields insists on the pleasure of your very selective
company . . . . The Sullivan-Vines at home . . . Hugo Kondratiuk
and Mickey Rourke's once-every-ten-year "what the hell" bash'.

Shag parties and stag parties may be fun, but they won't bestow
upon you any kind of credibility. Parties in warehouses and clubs
like the Limelight are not indicative of status either. Nor are the
'mega-groovy' Acid parties. A status party is not open to the

public, under any circumstances. It is private and very exclusive.
The various fashion and society mags have their opinions on which
parties are essential. Many status observers would argue, however, that attending any party where guests are pestered by
paparazzi for a society mag isn't a true indicator of status. Yet
there is definitely an inside track to be on with regard to party
status whether the event is chronicled or not. Provided you go to
your fair share of weekend house parties, charity and hunt balls,
wedding parties and drinks parties you're in with a chance.

Invites from the following are OK

Lord Glencommer (on Mustique)
The Marquis and Marchioness of Worcester – you remember
  Tracy Ward when she was Rachel Ward's baby sister
John Aspinall
Sir James Goldsmith
Mr and Mrs Robert Sangster
Prince and Princess Rupert Lowenstein
David and Carina Frost (but don't mention his recent job loss)
Mick and Jerry (they're well overdue for one)
Royals, particularly the Queen (one of the best of party-givers)
The Prime Minister (either at No. 10 or better still at a weekend
  at Chequers
Mrs Andrew Sinclair (Sonia Melchett)
Tina and Michael Chow (see 'the Tina Chow Set')
Karl Lagerfeld
People with Russian-sounding, unpronounceable surnames
A Guinness
A Rothschild
Lord Weidenfeld
Pierre Cardin
Marta Marzotto
Laurence 'Lorry' de Bras-Champ
The Sultan of Brunei
Charles Saatchi

Signs of a good status party

It lasts all weekend and you don't have to sleep at the local hotel.
You have to travel to another country to get there and the hostess
  simply isn't taking 'no' for an answer.

Though all sorts of grog are available (free, it goes without saying) it's not the object of the exercise to see how much regurgitated caviar you can propel across the neatly clipped lawns of your host.

Conversation is liberally peppered with talk about money (English companies buying up in a big way in the US), the Green Belt ('the new motorway backs on to my private trout stream, must have a word with the Transport Minister') and New York ('I'm sorry to miss the opening, but I'm in New York that week').

You don't necessarily recognize everyone: 'Oh, that's Calvin Klein. I thought he was much younger-looking.'

You meet girls with names like Katya, Tatanja and Sally-Anne.

You meet men with names like Jack and Armand and Misha.

Other guests tell you you've been conspicuous by your absence.

You hear someone say, 'Oh, Albert [Finney] has arrived. That should put the cat among the pigeons.'

Various big shots say to you, 'Isn't it about time you came and worked for me – whatever XYZ Corporation have offered you, I'll treble it.'

Someone whispers in your ear, 'Keep it under your hat, old chap, but I've heard very good things about Western Oil. I owed you one.'

As you leave, a Rothschild tells you to keep the 14th of next month free for his forthcoming party.

Signs of a bad status party
Queueing up for drink and food.
The drinks waiter is more popular than the so-called celebrities.
Queueing for the toilets because they're occupied by coke addicts.
Guests with names like Ringo, Boy, Del, Janine, Mandy, Bill, Rod, Bungalow, Janet and Jonathan.
You recognize a famous footballer and two Page Three girls.
Presenters from TV Arts programmes are in evidence.
Drugs, especially Ecstasy, are being discussed if not consumed.
You spot Peter Stringfellow.

Status is whose party you get invited to – in America

In the US, parties tend to be bigger and more often in the photographer's lens. The biggest and best are by invite only. *Town and Country* magazine chronicles many of them, while the exclusive private ones are only talked about enviously, weeks after the event. There is a mini-season in May, but the big events start in October, and run through till Christmas.

Charity is the big party industry in the US, and high society revolves around its money-generating circuit. Money buys social status when it's dumped in large wads into the coffers of some deserving trust. Patrons of the arts also score highly on the social status hit list: opera, theatre, ballet, museums and galleries. Apart from direct cash donations, galas are the main source of fundraising, and carry a great deal of cachet.

Openings at the Metropolitan Museum of Art in New York have status and an invitation to the opening night of Diana Vreeland's Costume Institute show in December is reputedly the highest honour a person can have in Manhattan. Opera balls in San Francisco, New York, Chicago and Washington are all pretty high up there on the list as well. *Here are some guests who may indicate you're at a heavy duty US status party*:

EAST COAST
The top fashion designers: Klein, Lauren, Blass
Top society ladies like Brooke Astor, Leonore Annenberg
Old showbiz folk like Frank and Barbara Sinatra, Bob Hope
The Kissingers
Betty Ford and Nancy Reagan
Cultured English Gents, (formerly it would have been David
    Niven)
Peggy Mulholland
Estée Lauder
Ann Getty
Mrs William Buckley
Paloma Picasso
Heavyweight writers: Saul Bellow, Norman Mailer, Don de Lillo,
    Gore Vidal, Joseph Heller
Carrie and Chris Pieroni
Peter Barnes (new wave English film director)

SIGN OF A BAD EAST COAST PARTY: YOU SPOT KLAUS VON BULOW

WEST COAST:

These parties are more movie and showbiz orientated like the party in *Annie Hall* given by Tony Lacey (Paul Simon), where a large proportion of the male faction are ageing, balding producers in search of finance to turn a concept into an idea before they go on to turn it into a film. The women tend to be lithe suntanned 'tens' with IQs to match.

West Coast showbiz parties carry far less status than their counterparts in the East. The same faces always tend to be in evidence: Sylvester Stallone, Eddie Murphy, Barbra Streisand, Cainey, the Gabor sisters. Private parties are held in restaurants like Spago's, Chinois on Main and The Bistro. Charity movie premieres like *Cheeseburger Hill* and *Out of Acton* are the standard events to enhance your status, but only in a minimal way.

The one and only party not to miss is Swifty Lazar's Oscar Night party in March. Anyone who is anyone will be there, from the youngest (Michael Jackson) to the oldest (George Burns).

SIGN OF A BAD WEST COAST PARTY: YOU SPOT AN INTELLECTUAL

PROFESSIONAL STATUS

What you do for a living, your work, your profession, can give you great status. Particularly among those mere mortals who find themselves only really working to live, rather than vice versa.

The status professions change all the time. The appeal of being an air stewardess, a *Playboy* bunny, a Bond girl, a matinee idol, a racing driver, a test pilot, a man from UNCLE, a playboy, a disc jockey, a TV evangelist, to name but a few, has shifted in favour of a glamour that is more solidly based on achievements, the work ethic and the profit incentive.

In recent times the status of the creative and media professions has increased greatly. Since Saatchi and Saatchi took the Conservative Party to two election successes, and later tried (albeit unsuccessfully) to take over one of the high street banks, advertising as a status profession, despite the current slump, has gone from strength to strength. Film and TV, meanwhile, continue to be significant industries status-wise. But it is the high fashion 'haute couture' industry with its huge returns and innate style that has superseded all others in the capitalist arena.

The City/Wall Street

Since the '88 Crash, the image of the City, particularly stocks and bonds dealers, has taken quite a bashing. The Boesky/Guinness scandal, and the fall of Michael Milken, the American Junk Bond King, did little to improve that image, though Boesky's alter ego, Gordon Gekko, in *Wall Street*, tried his best. Some of his lines, like, 'Lunch is for wimps,' and 'Greed is good' have become part of everyday conversation for some.

The problem is that the City and Wall Street environment is

only appealing if there are enormous amounts of money to be made. Currently there aren't. So the profession is in a bit of a lull. But it never lasts. Stocks and bonds dealers, if they survived the crash, can still dine out on stories of how much they made in 1986 and 1987, and of the concert parties and dawn raids they were involved in. The image of a wheeler and dealer is still an attractive one, and status is easily built on image.

With the recent *Capital City* TV series and programmes like *Chancer*, it's likely that City whizz-kid status will continue.

What about business generally?
The following are good signs of status:

Being your own boss

Being a tax exile

Owning your own multinational corporation

Having something called 'off-shore investments'

Being called 'a big player'

Being known as a 'corporate raider'

Taking over corporations that are hundreds of times bigger than your own (Martin Sorrell of WPP)

Being called an arbitrageur

Being a board director of several companies

And especially: moving out of something, just as everyone else is moving into it

Some other status professions

JOURNALISM: The old *Citizen Kane* (Randolph Hearst) or Lord Beaverbrook (*Daily Express*) image of running a newspaper doesn't work that well in the days of the tabloids, especially not for the likes of Eddie Shah. Nowadays the modern equivalent of Hearst Newspapers is a multi-media empire like Murdoch's and Maxwell's. Rank and file journalists' professional status depends on which papers and magazines they work for.

PUBLISHING: This is becoming a big status industry in the UK and already is a massive industry in the US: definitely one of the new status professions. The more status publishing has, the more status literary agents have too.

WRITER: This is getting higher and higher, especially for novelists since literary prizes were televised and publicized, like the Booker, and for biographers since Richard Ellman's massive success with *Oscar Wilde*. One of the ultimate American literary ambitions is (still) to write the Great American Novel, even though it has already been written many times. Screenplay writers have had status again since Lawrence (*The Big Chill*, *The Empire Strikes Back*) Kasdan appeared on the scene. A 'written and directed by' credit is a good one to have.

SCIENTIST: A new status career, ever since Stephen Hawking's book *A Brief History of Time* came out which made scientific theory accessible to all but a few lager louts and became an instant bestseller. Previously, scientific status was acknowledged only by other scientists.

ARTIST: Acclaim in your own lifetime brings mega-status and cash, for example Hockney, Bacon, Dali, Warhol.

ART GALLERY OWNER: Extremely big in the US, much less so in Britain. In fact, many London galleries are going bankrupt.

FOREIGN CORRESPONDENT: Ever since live newsreels showing real dangers to reporters were transmitted on prime-time TV, the status of foreign correspondents, for example Kate Adie, has risen to a height not enjoyed since Hitchcock's movie of the same name. War photographers also have great professional status, for example Don McCullin.

THE THEATRE: After a long period in the doldrums, when only Kenneth Tynan, Larry Olivier and Sir Peter Hall seemed to have any profile, the theatre is once again increasing in status. Kenneth Branagh (actor with his own theatre company) and Polly Davidson (stage manager) are two to mention.

FEMALE MODEL: If your face is the sole image of a perfume or fashion house, Isabella Rosellini (Lancôme), Carole Bouquet (Chanel), Ines de la Fressange, then your status is high. If you have been photographed by Richard Avedon or Irving Penn it's also high. If you've made it in New York, chances are it's high too. Page Three glamour is not where it's at.

NB: being a male model doesn't carry any status, though being a male nurse prepares you perfectly for winning a major literary prize (Paul Sayer, winner of the 1989 Whitbread Prize).

THE LAW: In its present form will always be a status profession. Being a female barrister carries particular high status. Hight Court judges are currently in the doghouse.

MEDICINE: Still high status, much more on the hospital side than general practice, and particularly surgeons and psychiatrists.

POP STAR: Far less status than formerly. Where once it was the ultimate status profession back in the days of Beatlemania, these days it's more of a job than an exercise in deification.

SURVEYOR: Apart from the effort, of Michael Ridley and Robert Pugh to give the profession a more glamorous profile, the day of the surveyor has yet to come.

PROFESSIONAL CHESS PLAYER: A great indicator of childhood status. The younger the champion, the better. And a great indicator of older, more intellectual status, especially if you beat a Russian.

A PRIVATE DETECTIVE WITH A PRIVATE INCOME AND A SILLY SIDEKICK: Sherlock Holmes, Hercule Poirot, etc.: such a wonderful leisurely status existence. Always neatly solving the plot just in time for tea, and always time for a quick quip to keep the lower orders happy.

Unemployment

It's not terrifically status to be out of work even if it isn't your fault. If you're out of work, a book on status is probably low on your list of priorities anyway. If it's any consolation, it's more status to be out of work than a clamper of cars.

Admired by their peers

John Webster (advertising)
Ben Leven (artist)
Dean Richards (rugby union)
Sir John Hicks (economist)
Peter Brook (theatre director)
Keith Waterhouse (newspaper columnist)
Michael Buerk (newscaster)
Ian McEwan (novelist)
Peter Scudamore (jockey)
Alain Prost (formula one driver)
Sir David English (editor)

Bryony Brind (ballet dancer)
Alasdair MacIntyre (philosopher)
Olivier Messiaen (composer)
Henri Cartier-Bresson (photographer)
Herbert Von Karajan (late-conductor)
Sir Patrick Moore (astronomer)
Lord Denning (former judge and Master of the Rolls)
John Coltrane (jazz musician)
Pierre Koffmann (chef)

(Source: *The Observer* magazine)

Lloyd's (any time you're flush)

The rich, the royal and the famous have been doing it for years – Earl Westmorland, Princess Alexandra, Princess Michael of Kent, Virginia Wade, Adam Faith, Pink Floyd, to name a few. If you've got a spare £100,000 knocking around you might like to join the queue for Lloydsamoney of London – the high-status, high-risk way to lose your shirt. Just as the Stock Exchange is a market for buying and selling financial securities, so Lloyds is a market for buying and selling risk. Get it right and you can make a fortune, get it wrong and it's time to start selling the heirlooms.

Yet Lloyd's position as a status institution has recently taken a severe bashing. In the wake of the Piper Alpha claim (only earthquakes and hurricane claims have come to more), the recent boom in membership looks set to slump. Their tax perks gone, Lloyd's 'names', who stake their all in the bespoke insurance market, are demanding a safer run for their money.

Also affecting Lloyd's long record as a status institution, are a series of well-publicized scandals that have hit it in the last ten years and have tarnished its reputation, particularly in the US – Cameron Webb, Sasse, Goldfinger Postgate, Peter Dixon.

The feeling among status observers at present is that it's best to take a back seat for the time being, at least until things cool down. If you've got a spare £100,000, and you want to spend it on a status institution with a rapid appreciation, spend it on a Ferrari.

Fashion designer – a big status profession

Remember, when asked by the teacher at school what he wanted to be when he grew up, the bespectacled artistic kid who announced he wanted to be a clothes designer, and later got his testicles removed in the playground by his classmates for having such a sissy ambition? Well . . .

Over the past few years, fashion designers have turned hems and shoulder pads into Palladian palazzi, châteaux, Louis XV furniture, Lear Jets and private islands. Some have become richer than whole countries, and many have fortunes that are already outstripping those of the hotel and motor car industries. Like the great cotton barons of nineteenth-century Manchester who endured ten years of anxiety before their investments became good, the designer billionaires who have survived this far have seen the momentum of their businesses become too strong for them to falter. Fashion designers are either Division One or Two. But either will do to ensure status.

DIVISION ONE DESIGNERS

Ralph Lauren, richest of US designers (1986 turnover around $1.3 billion)

Calvin Klein, second richest of US designers

Georgio Armani (Italy), pretty damn rich

Pierre Cardin (France), 'Moi aussi.'

Louis Feraud (France), 'Et moi.'

Valentino (France), 'Et moi.'

Gianni Versace (Italy), 'Mia too.'

Liz Claiborne (US), 'And me.'

Yves St Laurent (France), 'Keeps me in spectacles.'

Karl Lagerfeld (France), 'No comment.'

Emanuel Ungaro (France), 'No comment.'

Oscar de la Renta (Italy), 'How you say? It pays the renta.'
Bill Blass (US), 'No comment.'

DIVISION TWO
Krizia, Beene, Givenchy, Montana, Ferre, the Missonis, Laura
    Biagiotti.

Apart from the stylish method by which they earn their money,
it's the way the fashion designers dispose of it that gives them such
incredibly high status. For example: Lauren has a 10,000-acre
ranch in Colorado, a Fifth Avenue duplex in New York, a beach
front home on Long Island, a holiday home in Montego Bay in
Jamaica. Klein has his Central Park West duplex with its collection
of Georgia O'Keefe paintings, and houses in Key West and on
Fire Island. Yves St Laurent has a fabulous art collection. Karl
Lagerfeld has a network of homes across Europe and lives in the
manner of an eighteenth-century marquis. His heirs are a closely
guarded secret.

In Italy, where Armani, Versace and Valentino are already
approaching the Agnelli league, a standard Milanese inventory is
a heavily frescoed palazzo, an island off Capri, Sardinia or Sicily,
a huge power or sail boat to visit it in, and a weekend house on
Lake Como or Mortlake.

For anyone thinking of going into the fashion business, remember most of the big successes have had an astute business partner
behind them. And in the case of Karl Lagerfeld a cute little
ponytail as well.

THE STATUS OF BODY LANGUAGE

Body language, like everything else, is a great indicator of status. How you move on the dance floor. The way you walk into a room, confidently, as if you owned the place. How you sit in Concorde, straight or slumped, legs casually crossed. How strong and gracefully you swim. How confidently you smile. How manfully you rub your chin. How melodiously you laugh. Your regal brow. Your stiff upper lip. Your perfect white teeth. Your deep voice. Your piercing eyes looking directly into someone else's. Everything, right down to the way you make a ritual of putting on your spectacles to look at a menu in an exclusive restaurant, and take them off again once you've made your choice – 'We'll have the lobster, a green salad and a bottle of '61. Now where were we?' All these are signs or indications of possible status, and, equally, all ways in which you may also betray your status.

How you present yourself, in every minute detail, is what status observers look for when making an assessment. A chewed nail, a fleck of dandruff, a stray bogey, and you could blow the whole thing. The way you dress (see p. 79) is also essential.

The body in question

BREATH: Good breath is taken for granted. Bad, or dog breath is an indicator of low status, followed by rotten teeth and unwashed hair.

FINGERNAIL BITING: Occasionally permissible in tense situations, though preferably faked rather than visibly consumed.

ACNE: Plain bad luck but does, in some cases, indicate underlying artistic sensitivity or scientific or boffin potential. If in doubt, grow a beard. If a woman, try either a head transplant or an expensive Swiss clinic for a cure.

FARTING: No status potential whatsoever, except perhaps in France (e.g. Joseph Pujol, the famous French anal impressionist, whose extraordinary farting talents made him a genuine *fin de siècle* superstar, topping the bill at the Moulin Rouge for years).

BELCHING: Not really, except perhaps when registering extreme boredom or cheating at bridge.

HYSTERICAL SCREAMING: No place in the status view of life, but weeping or crying is OK, provided it's dignified and silent.

SMALL NEAT SCARS: On men these increase their status with women, but rarely vice versa.

LOVE BITES: Strictly high school status.

MASTURBATION: Won't prejudice your status as long as it's not done in public.

THE GREAT TITS DEBATE: Cleavage once had high status (Sophia Loren, Raquel Welch, Monroe, Bardot), then it disappeared for a long time in favour of skinny 32B mannequins, but is now making a comeback (Beatrice Dalle).

MALE APPENDAGES: The larger variety are generally considered to offer their owners greater status, provided they know what to do with them. Those who violently disagree with this theory probably have good reason to.

HAIR: Has always been a status manifestation, though some styles, for example perms, relegate their owners, men and women, instantly to the fourth division. The skinhead crop is of debatable status since no one in their right mind is going to argue the toss with one of those fine gentlemen: 'I may have no status in your view, but I think these steel-capped Dr Martens say different, don't you, Mr Softy Intellectual cringing there in the corner?'

Nowadays short, long, shaved or bald styles are all permissible, so long as they are clean and well cut.

CHINS: Can't be 'weak'. They should either be cleanshaven or bearded. Designer stubble is strictly male model these days, for example George Michael and Rupert Everett.

MODEL BODIES: Having stepped out from the magazine covers into the real world, model bodies will flounder and be in danger of ending up merely as a status symbol on the end of someone's chubby, but well-tailored arm, if they have nothing to say for themselves but 'uh?' and 'uh huh'.

BEAUTY AND BRAINS: Together they are reasonably rare, so concomitant status is very high. (For example Candice Bergen, Jane Fonda, Harrison Ford, Robert Kilroy Silk.)

HANDWRITING: A great indicator of status, but no one can tell whether it should be neat or erratic (look at doctors). In which case, the content, vocabulary and spelling should all be scrutinized. A cool, fabby long looping signature is a must status-wise. And lots of extra points if you're left-handed.

VOCABULARY: The more, the more.

BLOOD GROUP: Donate some blood, discover your blood group and then boast that you have a rare group to all your friends if it's anything but O positive (the most common type). Alternatively, you can get involved in a road accident where you subsequently require a blood transfusion, tell the paramedic your rare blood type and watch him nod sorrowfully as he says, 'There's none readily available' and proceeds to give you the last rites.

DRESS STATUS

The way you dress is a very important indicator of your status. There are a few general rules:

1. Dressing fashionably is a good status sign, but being a fashion slave is definitely not.

2. Appearing on a 'best-dressed' list is not the ultimate status accolade, but everyone (especially Japanese fashion designers with their hari-kari knives poised) waits with baited breath every year for Eleanor Lambert to circulate her choice.

3. To be able to say, 'I never wear the same thing twice' is indeed a sign of status, but it'll cost you an even greater fortune finding space for those walnut wardrobes.

4. It's very important not to look as if you've tried too hard with clothes. Enhancing certain of your body's more favourable features is important so long as it's subtle, for example backless dresses rather than crotchless panties.

5. Finally it's not so much a matter of good dressing equalling status, as bad dressing equalling low status or none at all.

THE BEST OF THE REST

Owning your own DJ/tuxedo: essential for status

Having your own personal tailor: ditto

Materials are all-important: natural fibres, like cotton, wool, silk, cashmere as opposed to nylon, polyester

Grey shoes are practically the lowest form of status there is. Training shoes and pumps as casual wear are not far behind. Only well-cobbled leather footwear will do

Avoid clip-on bow-ties at all costs

Your own clothes designs could be a great sign of status, depending on how they look

Brown suits for men are generally a thumbs-down

Braces are status if they're the button type. The clip-on variety are a sign of great inferiority

Uniforms are far less status than they used to be, even in time of war

Aftershaves and perfumes can either be a sign of status or a sign of extreme unsociability

SOME MEN WHO GET AWAY WITH DRESSING BADLY: David Bailey, Van Morrison, Alan Whicker, Bob Dylan (who said Michael Foot?).

SOME WOMEN WHO GET AWAY WITH DRESSING BADLY: None.

Speech, accent and language

The way you talk. The depth of your voice. How much you say.
How much you keep to yourself. How many languages you speak.
The way you deliver an argument. Your humour. Your ability to
pluck out of the blue the right verses, quotes and quotations. The
way you speak from knowledge and experience. Your analytical
powers. Your choice of topics of conversation. In fact, everything
that comes out of your mouth, apart from spit, sick and garlic
breath, adds to or detracts from your status.

ROLE MODELS: Oscar Wilde for speaking in perfectly constructed
sentences. Dorothy Parker for the put-down. Clint Eastwood for
minimalist speech. Shakespeare for his prose. Yeats for his poetry.
Laurence Olivier for his delivery. Max Headroom for his distinc-
tive difference. Meryl Streep for her accents.

THE RIGHT LANGUAGES: Russian, French, Japanese, Gaelic, Por-
tuguese, Chinese, Rain Forest Indian.

THE WRONG LANGUAGES: Misuse of English, Franglais, Geordie,
Pidgin Chinese, South Efrican Impressions of a Yorkshireman.

Toilet or not toilet – a guide to conversational status
What you call 'the little room' is a very good indicator of status
conversation-wise. 'Lavatory', 'loo', 'the plumbing', 'the bathroom', 'the rest room', even 'the bog' are all permitted. 'Toilet' is
not a word people with status use. Neither is 'gents', 'crapper' or
'turd shed'. If you feel yourself tempted to ask where 'the
shithouse might possibly be located' in polite company, think very
carefully, especially if you're seriously thinking of asking Melissa's
pater for Melissa's hand.

Other conversational indicators
Name-dropping, verbal one-upmanship, the economical put-
down, a sharp tongue, creative insults, sneers and slighs: are all

OBITUARIES

J. C. TREWIN

with the biggest memory bank of them

dramatic critic Birmingham Post.

He was as active in ism - which over the y included many pieces Times - as he was pr the writing of book interspersed his stud plays and biographies o ers with literary retur Cornwall for his biographical Up From Lizard and his antholog West Country Book. Alth John Trewin was fon listing "All things Cur under the head "Recreation" in Who's he stayed away from county for many years an was only quite recently tha derived pleasure fr rediscovering the part Britain in which he grew up

The theatre which sto highest in his affection w that at Stratford-upon-Avc and he was joint historia with T.C.Kemp in 1953 of th annual Shakespeare Festiva there. He frequently contrib uted to the history of the drama in all its aspects from the eccentric to the sublime. book was the

known more justly, as "actor's critic" because vast memory of performar especially in the classical ertoire, allowed him to comparisons and to know how demanding - or e each role was.

Towards the end of b J.C.Trewin was asked w he sometimes got bore the theatre. He might have answered that the reply was contained in the title of his last major book, Five and Eighty Hamlets. But that was not his sort of reply. He said, instead, that he went each night to the theatre with a feeling of expectation and hope that when the house lights went down "something interesting was going to happen." That enthusiasm, inevitably not al ways well placed, shone through his reviews. Joh Trewin rarely miss portant open found

and of its peted people. Later in his life, from 1951 to 1957, he was the enthusiastic editor of The West Country Magazine.

After his education at Plym outh College he started his career as a journalist in that city, aged 18, working for The Western Independent. Hi long-continued dedi the theatre h bec

freelance. He became contributor to The Observer, joining the staff and remain ing there during the Second World War since he for militar book

when he was elect ent ritic's Club in 1964. the plays night after a daily paper is work which can freshness of ap theatre. But with rience his judg ened and hard-

PEOPLE WITH STATUS

Above left: Frank Sinatra's number-one rule about top status: 'To achieve it, you gotta do it My Way'

Above right: The world's most elegantly wasted human being? Keith Richard champions the status of the unhealthy by his continued high-octane existence

Left: Robert de Niro, generally regarded as the 'actor's actor'. To get de Niro to make a cameo appearance in your film is a sign of status – Alan Parker (*Angel Heart*), Brian de Palma (*The Untouchables*)

Below: Samuel Beckett – 'Status is absurd. Give me a pint of French beer any day'

Above: Harold Evans and Tina Brown. At first he gave her status. Then she gave him status. Who's on the end of your arm is a very significant pointer of status

Top right: The male Top Status award, 1990. Gianni Agnelli, boss of Fiat, basks in its rarefied atmosphere

Below: A rare combination of beauty and intelligence, Catherine Deneuve has the status of being the most celebrated woman in France and is the epitome of Euro-chic

Above: Despite naming all his possessions after himself (Trump Tower, Trump Plaza, Trump Princess, Ivana), Donald Trump retains his status having bought up the copyright to that particular word

STATUS SYMBOLS

Above: Owning your own island, like Marlon Brando or Ian Anderson of Jethro Tull, is status indeed. If you've got one without phones or communication with the outside world, all the more so

Opposite above: A Ferrari. Not a Testarossa; not a limited edition F40 or GTO; but a cool sophisticated Berlinetta Boxer 512, *circa* 1976–84

Opposite below: A Harley-Davidson, the only motorcycle to ride for status. In the event of an accident, the injured party makes their way to a similarly named street for private medical attention

DECADES OF STATUS

Above: 1940s status – kills chalked up on the fuselage. In World War II, everyone scrambled for this particular type of wartime status

Right: 1960s status. London was *the* place to be in the swinging sixties. To be like Jean Shrimpton was a model of 1960s status. Jean quit while she was on top, thus ensuring her permanent status

Left: 1970s status. Playboy culture, glamorized by James Bond and Hugh Heffner, was once high status. It went out, never to return, at the tail-end of the 1970s

Below: 1980s status – the Tina Chow set. Tina Chow, Queen of the Tina Chow set, and her husband Mr Chow, the internationally famous restaurateur, were the 'set' to be among in the 1980s. They seek her here . . . They seek her there . . .

STATUS EVENTS

Above: Ascot – a great status event. See the punters discussing the form before the race in the car park

Left: The Americas Cup, currently one of the top status events on the planet. Only the mega-rich and powerful need apply

Below: Polo. Royals do it; lords and ladies do it; the international money set do it. Polo is a far nicer way of doing battle with Argentinians. And so much more sporting!

tricks to advertise status by word or sound of mouth. But, more often than not, it is the nature of your conversation that will ultimately determine your status.

'God, make me a tax exile, but not yet,' is an indicator of status.

'Isn't *Brookside* on the other Channel?' is not.

'He dropped 30,000 in Monty, but didn't bat an eyelid,' is.

'I'm a bit skint right now,' is not.

'Life is rather splendid, isn't it?' is.

'Phew, what a scorcher,' isn't.

Over the moon *Sun*speak isn't. Top notch *Time*speak could be. At the end of the day you'll know it when you hear it.

Manners

Manners maketh man. But sometimes bad manners are an equally big sign of status, for example when putting down your host in public or at a dinner party when they have done you an injustice and believe they can get away with it simply because of the fact that you're in a public place or large gathering. Most good dramas usually have a scene or two where this occurs, e.g. *Inadmissible Evidence* by John Osborne.

Attraction to the opposite sex

Being attractive (not attracted) to the opposite sex carries very high status indeed. Ever since adolescence, the ease with which the odd few enjoyed such success with the opposite sex was a subject of eternal fascination and envy to the spotty, gangly, awkward rest of us, who naturally took our opportunities with whomever we could, in whatever shape or state, and were grateful for the chance.

It was ironic that the only people who thought nought of their luck and success were those few men and women who seemed to enjoy an endless conveyor belt of admiring bimbos and beefcaked hunks yet who (so they maintained) would have gladly swapped a few days of peace in place of the tiresome advances of their beautiful moonstruck conquests. Like hell, we countered. Like hell.

As we grew up, however, we learnt, much to our relief, that 'looks aren't everything' and that 'beauty is only skin deep'. And that much of what constituted one's attraction was often indefinable or vague, or many things rolled into one. This made us very pleased indeed, and we told ourselves that we always knew there was a place for the conker champion and the embroidery queen of Class 4A.

We learnt, for example, that it was attractive to be funny, or to be clever, or to have money, or to be powerful or anarchic or independent along with several other attributes flaunted in lonely hearts advertisements, like 'sensitive' and 'gentle' and 'caring', as opposed to simply having great physical attributes. You didn't have to be a ten. You could be an extremely humorous four who could have them rolling in the aisles (and under your duvet) with your surpassingly witty Arthur Scargill impersonations. Ultimately, whatever it is that makes one attractive to the opposite sex, not once, but over and over again, is still a rare thing and therefore carries high status.

Sexual Status
Once it was status to be virgin until marriage, virginity a valuable prize to capture (cf. Brooke Shields in the film *Pretty Baby*). Once it was status to be a stud of the Warren Beatty type. (NB: Sir Ralph Halpern didn't do too badly out of it recently.) Though it was never status to be a nymphomaniac, to be able to satisfy one certainly was (sexist or what?). It was rarely status to remain celibate (sorry, Cliff). Bisexuality was given status by David Bowie for about ten minutes in the seventies. Sex symbols were the thing to be in the sixties. Multiple marriages were popularized by Elizabeth Taylor and Zsa Zsa Gabor. Nowadays it's sexual status just to be alive and kicking, with a ton of shares in Wellcome or London Rubber.

Single status
Frequently the state that is regarded as having a touch more status, though this will entirely depend on the context. Naturally if you're the international arriviste with the solo pad, and enjoy plenty of independence, variety and an unencumbered career, being single is a good idea, especially if the gossip columns hang

an 'extremely eligible' tag on you. Single status is pretty zero status, however, if you're living on an Orkney island with only one available woman, twelve available men and several sexually ambivalent sheep.

The economics of demand and supply come into operation with regard to the status of the single condition, which tends to be inversely related to availability of the opposite sex. In New York City, single heterosexual men enjoy a high status rating, since there are allegedly three times as many single women as men. 'Er, yeah, Kimberley, I'd like to see you this weekend, but I'm taking the whole of the Elite Model Agency out on a nature ramble.' In London, even though there is a more even balance between the sexes, it seems to be higher status to be in a couple. It tends to be so much more convenient for dinner parties.

Married status
The big wedding. No expense spared. Limos and Louis Roederer aplenty. All your favourite people. The photographers from *Tatler* and *Vanity Fair*. The exotic honeymoon destination. The uniting of two great families. A cake bigger than the Chrysler Building. Trendy registry office ceremony followed by church white with papal blessing. Your godfather receiving guests in the main house. The perfect couple both in your public and social life. The perfect match, destined to produce perfect children who will take over the reins of the family corporation as you develop into the perfect dynasty. Or . . .

Had to get married, kid followed kid, career took a nose dive, cash-flow problems, looks fading fast, figure gone to bits, turned to drink, waited five years before filing for divorce, by which time no one wanted to know me.

Or somewhere in between.

CONCLUSION: Some marriages are made in heaven, some in Sellafield.

HEALTH AND WEALTH

Wealth

It's status to have wealth because wealth can open so many doors and simply buy you all the status you want. Of course you have to have the necessary knowledge and insight about the right things to invest it in or spend it on. It's no status at all to spend it on thousands of pairs of shoes, or bottles of extremely expensive wines (once the effects of the first few have erased your memory banks). Likewise, it's important that the slightly less ephemeral objects you spend your money on – paintings, antiques, etc. – will stand up to public approbation rather than ridicule.

Everyone knows that some three-eyed old hag strumming a guitar by Picasso is a reasonable status symbol to own. Everyone knows how to play the 'if I had a million quid, I'd know how to spend it really stylishly' game, but only a few of us can play the game for real. The rest of us sit on the touchlines waiting for the real players to make some terrible faux pas with their purchases, like our lady of conspicuous consumption, Imelda Marcos. Spending or investing vast pots of money on the wrong things can totally negate any status you might have had.

The status of wealth is all about the exclusivity of it, its sheer power and how well you hang on to it. Money is the perfect status currency even though it's not the only one.

Few of us have the drive or the capabilities to make real wealth. Even the few who do, the few who succeed now face a new hurdle because it's no longer status to be a millionaire. Today you have to be a billionaire to warrant true status.

The billionaires club

Yep, I guess you could call it status to be a billionaire. Billionaires aren't exactly two a penny like millionaires. In fact 1988 recorded

129 individuals and families on the old 'Billy' list. The good news is that you don't have to be an octogenarian eccentric reclusive fart to be one, either. The kid next door has now become eligible. The youngest billionaire is one William H. Gates II (note the neat 'Billy-type' name) who is currently in his thirties. Billy co-founded and owns 40 per cent of the software producer Microsoft. His wealth in 1988 was estimated at $1.4 billion. How did he do it? In tenth grade he made $20,000 by developing a computer program that plotted traffic patterns in Seattle. He dropped out of Harvard to co-found Microsoft. And the rest just followed good old market forces.

The top Billys

1. The Sultan of Brunei. $25 billion. Oil. Being the top Billy naturally gives old Hassanal the added status of being the richest person in the world.

2. King Fahd Bin Abdul Aziz Al Saud and family. $18 billion. Oil. A model of Islamic propriety since assuming the throne in 1982.

3. Forrest E. Mars and family. $12.5 billion. The richest family in the US thanks to the Mars Bar among other things.

4. Queen Elizabeth II. $8.7 billion. Nice to see a Brit in there.

5. Mitzi Newhouse and family. $8.7 billion. 100 per cent of Advance publications and Newhouse broadcasting.

6. Sam Moore Walton and family. $7.4 billion. 39 per cent of Wal-Mart Stores.

7. Albert Reichmann and family. $6.3 billion. Canada's richest family. They control more than 45 million square feet of office space in the US and Canada.

8. Kenneth Colin Irving and family. $6.2 billion. Three sons nicknamed Gassy, Oily and Greasy. Nuff said.

9. Kenneth (popular name for a Billy it would seem) R. Thomson. $6.0 billion. The Thomson organization.

10. Gerald Grosvenor, Duke of Westminster and family. $5.4

billion. Britain's richest man. 300 acres of upper crust Belgravia and Mayfair districts amongst other investments.

11. The Wang family. $4.6 billion. The largest conglomerate in Taiwan and the world's largest producer of resins.

12. Queen Beatrix of Holland. $4.4 billion. A queen-size portfolio, including stock in Shell.

13. Sid Richardson Bass and brothers. $4.0 billion. Sid Richardson Senior was a legendary Texas wildcatter like old Jock Ewing and Digger Barnes. He gave most of his money to nephew Perry Bass and his four sons. One of these sons, Sid Junior, got an MBA from Stanford in 1968, took control of the fortune, and ran it into billions by plunging into oil and real estate. So if you see Sid . . .

14. Sheikh Jaber Ahmed Al Sabah and family of Kuwait. $4.0 billion. You guessed it – oil.

15. Jay Arthur and Robert Alean Pritzker and family. $3.5 billion. Chicago. Major ownership of the Hyatt Hotel chain.

16. Johanna Quandt and family. $3.5 billion. West Germany. 70 per cent of BMW.

17. Godfried Brenninkmeyer. $3.4 billion. Holland. Major shareholder in C&A retail stores. Follows the dictum that 'secrecy is good policy.'

18. Gad and Hans Rausing. $3.3 billion. England. Major interest in Tetra Pak, one of the world's largest liquid food packagers.

19. John Werner Kluge. $3.1 billion. USA. Holds 97.4 per cent of Metromedia Co.

20. Walter H. Annenberg. $3.0 billion. USA. Triangle publications.

21. Edgar M. Bronfman and Charles R. Bronfman and family. $3.0 billion. They hold 38 per cent of Seagram Co. Distillers. Founded in Montreal during Prohibition. Wonder if they knew the Kennedys?

22. Henry Lea Hillman. $3.0 billion. USA. Real estate.

23. Charles and David Koch. $3.0 billion. USA. Koch Industries: oil, gas, real estate.

24. Various Sainsburys. $3.0 billion. England. They hold 50 per cent of Sainsbury's, Britain's largest grocery chain.

25. A. Alfred Taubman. $3.0 billion. USA. Real estate. Yawn.

SOME OF THE REST ($ billions): The Benetton family ($1.0), Kerry Packer ($1.1), Baron Thyssen ($1.2), Sir James Goldsmith ($1.2), Robert Maxwell ($1.4), Rupert Murdoch ($1.4), Donald Trump ($1.3), Giovanni Agnelli ($1.5), Josephine and William Clay Ford ($2.0), Estee Lauder and family ($1.8), William and Randolph Hearst ($1.6), Freddy Heineken ($1.3), G. P. Getty ($1.2), 4th son of J. Paul Getty.

Inexpensive ways to improve your status
Joey Boswell carries it off with panache in the soap *Bread*. Despite the fact that he's unemployed, his shining bright twenty-year-old Mark 2 Jaguar is a status symbol that places him above the rest, unemployed or not. Joey's car says more about Joey than 'bread' ever can, and you'll notice it's not even the 3.8-litre variety. Some others include:

● The *Financial Times* (45p) 'Look at that guy. He's only wearing jeans and a bomber jacket. But wait, what's that under his arm? The instantly recognizable pink pages of the *FT*. Cripes, he must in actual fact be one of those "I-don't-care-how-I-look-so-long-as-I-make-a-killing-on-the-stock market type bond dealers". What a cool dude. What style! What status!'
(NB: it doesn't even have to be today's *FT*, so long as you carry one around with you. Price from the rubbish bin? Zilch.)

● Buy one share (a couple of pounds). You can tell people, 'I dabble in the stock market.'

● Learn backgammon/bridge/chess (free). These are all status games. You're on a Greek beach, the owner of your favourite bar challenges you to a game. You beat him and all his hirsute friends. Aristotle Onassis's less famous, but equally rich, distant cousin hears of your exploits and invites you to dinner aboard his yacht. There you meet the beautiful and well-connected Melissa, who has other games in mind. (NB: similar happy endings for bridge and chess.)

- Take up oil painting (cheap). It doesn't matter how bad you are. It doesn't even matter if you can't paint at all. Just add a couple of blobs of paint to a canvas and you can tell *tout le monde*, 'I paint.' Watch the unartistic fraternity turn green with envy. Watch the art dealers' eyes turn green with potential dollar signs.

- Have in your threadbare wardrobe one decent suit or outfit (average cost £300). One good suit or outfit has status written all over it, far more than several items of cheaper clothing. A decent whistle still opens doors, even if it is only at the local Palais de Danse.

- Move into your own flat (not too crippling depending on which area you choose and absolutely free if it's a squat in Belgravia). There's nothing wrong with living with your parents, but it could have its problems: 'Yeah, I'd like to invite you back to my place for coffee, Mick and Jerry, but my Dad doesn't like people coming around after twelve.'

- Buy an old Citroen 2CV (c. £200–£500). There aren't many convertibles you can acquire so cheaply. 2CVs still carry a lot of inverted status.

- Learn a foreign language (cost – time). Fluency in a language other than English (though it also carries a lot of status to speak English well) carries a lot of clout both at home and abroad, since the English are notoriously bad at other languages.

- Read some of the great philosophers (cost – time). Interspersing your conversation with odd quotes and words of wisdom from old Freddy Nietzsche or Manny Kant will guarantee you a rapt audience among your fellow Friday night diners at the local Taj Mahal Curry House.

- Change your name (free). Bye Bye, Aristotle and Doreen Implant. Hello, Maxwell and Selena Greatly-Improved.

- Buy your weekly shopping from Harrods' food halls (cost – more than you'd normally pay from the supermarket. Probably less than you'd pay from the corner shop). Exchange grumblings about the upward spiralling price of fresh lobster with Princess Michael, Susan Hampshire and Bob Hoskins.

- Hire a KORG M1 (cost – £75.00 a day). Compose, record and re-record a concept album in the space of an afternoon.

- Adopt foibles (free). Like drinking an unusual drink, wearing an exciting outfit to a funeral, making your eyeballs roll in their sockets, smoking three cigarettes at the same time.

- Pick up book-matches of famous restaurants and bars without dining or drinking at them (free). Light Melissa's cigarette and hear her say: 'My God, you've been to Spago's. You're obviously not the three-time-loser I took you for.'

- Make the slow transformation from lager (absolutely no status) to beer (indifferent status) to mineral water (status).
  If you have to drink alcohol, drink neat vodka.

- Invest in private medical insurance (cost – c. £300 per annum). And then deliberately go out and catch something nasty so you can tell all your friends to visit you in a swish hospital.

- Leave second-hand copies of Sotheby's and Christie's catalogues lying around.

- Cancel your subscription to *Amateur Photographer* (save – pounds, and lots of face).

- Give all of your nylon shirts to Oxfam (they're the second lowest form of male apparel this century, after grey shoes).

- Fill in your cheque-book stubs with fabricated purchases, for example, Lear Jet, £38,000,000 (cost – a few drops of ink).

Health status

Health clubs. No more smoking, low-fat, semi-skimmed diets. 'Look at my pecs.' 'Sorry I can't make the big poker game tonight,

I've got to work out.' It's status to be healthy nowadays. Health
clubs are the places where the upwardly mobiles go to meet other
upwardly mobiles to compare and contrast racket ability, weight-
lifting capacity and, most importantly, to pick up insider trading
tips, while semi-obscured in the steam bath.

The more you pay for your exclusive club membership, the
more you like it.

If your club is called 'The Downtown' or the 'Uptown Racquet
Club' or has the name 'Racquet' somewhere in the title, then it
has status. These days it's no longer enough to say that you're a
member of the squash club, or the tennis club.

Overall it's status to live a long and full life, to be a picture of
Dorian Gray, with your gleaming white teeth, full head of hair
(albeit steely grey) and your faculties intact till it's time to shuffle
off the mortal coil. It's status to age gracefully and still be able to
go a few sets of tennis with Bjorn without inducing cardiac arrest.

By the same token, being extremely unhealthy or in bad health
can give people great status too.

Unhealthy status

It's status to live a long unhealthy life, have fun doing it, and defy
all the odds of making it to octogenarian status. Winston Churchill
did it. Keith Richards is well on the way.

People tend to relate to unhealthy movie characters like Mickey
Rourke and Tom Waits who seem to survive despite constant
injections of nicotine and cheeseburgers. The gross and appropri-
ately named hero in Martin Amis's novel *Money*, John Self, was
certainly someone who ran on heavy fuel, but who, despite his
vile habits, came across as an appealing character because of his
instinct for survival.

Stressful jobs tend to be the ones that carry most status, where
workaholic is not a dirty word, rather a symbol of admiration: all
those cigarettes, pills, black coffee and alcoholic lunches that keep
the addicted driving on; those meetings that go on through the
night with no sleep; the early morning plane to catch; the criss-
crossing of cabs and choppers across town and between sky-
scrapers to deliver high energy executives to high level meetings

to deliver high level decisions. Where the doctor advises, 'Cut down and take it easy' as he puts the mercury-splattered blood pressure kit to one side . . .

The image has been established through countless movies where private detectives of the Marlowe ilk live without sleep, a bottle of rye in their pockets, and chain-smoking air traffic controllers with loosened tie and rolled up shirtsleeves always bring the crippled aircraft in to land.

Status illnesses and afflictions
Paranoia
Extremely rare diseases (so rare, in fact, that you're the only person in the world to suffer the symptoms)
High blood pressure
Insomnia
Migraines and assorted headaches
Yuppie flu
The dealing-room coke snuffle
Fear and loathing
Stabs in the back
A bullet lodged in your side as you continue to solve a crime without seeking treatment

Sure it's status to live a long, healthy life, but if you can't manage that, it's better to die now, have a good-looking corpse, and enter the status elite of those who died young, unfulfilled and immortalized for all time: the Jimmy Deans, Buddy Hollys and Jimi Hendrixes of this world.

Private medicine
Yes, it's status to have several personal doctors in Harley Street. But do they drop everything and hurry to your bedside whenever you have a sniffle? Probably.

Smooth operators – some status hospitals in London
The Cromwell
The Humana
The Portland
The London Clinic

The Princess Grace
The Fitzroy Nuffield
The Garden Hospital
The King Edward VII

A status drug rehabilitation clinic
Broadway Lodge, Weston-super-Mare (Cecil Parkinson's daughter Mary went there).

A US clinic of noted status
The Betty Ford Clinic (all the stars go there, including Ringo).

INTERNATIONAL STATUS

Status doesn't always cross frontiers. What might constitute absolutely no status back home, in another country might be big status indeed due to its scarcity value. For example hairy chests are no big deal in most countries (at least not on men) but in Japan, where the males aren't remotely hirsute, an abundance of hair could be a status symbol. (Rumour has it that the Japanese are not very big on the male appendage side either, so even averagely endowed Westerners are looked on with some envy, as Ransom, the hero of Jay McInerney's novel of the same name, finds out when he visits his local Kyoto steam bath.)

Western pop music culture travels eastwards well. And various aspects of Japanese history (the Samurai), interior decor (sparse), food (sushi) and manners have all been admired in the West at one time or another.

Italian design travels well, as do French food and fashions. And while the British seem to have been buying up big US corporations (Pillsbury, Brooks Brothers, J. Walter Thompson, Saks 5th Avenue), they seem to be leaving a lot of English culture behind them at the same time.

The person who seems to be well versed in what constitutes status within individual countries, and flexible enough to adapt to it without losing his own individual status as a foreigner (you don't have to spit on trains, but you should learn the language), is on the way to achieving international status.

United Status

Big cars. Fat cigars. An ever-ready carpet-width roll of dollar bills. Diamond necklaces and furs for the molls who stare adoringly into the eyes of their Al Capone-type boyfriends. A country full of big tycoons, big daddies, big John Waynes and the tallest buildings in the world. These are just some of the images that make their way across the Atlantic via out-of-date TV, films and sub-standard satirical shows. A foreigner's view of what constitutes American status.

It is true that an American perception of status differs from our own and the rest of Europe's. (Britain still doesn't consider itself to be part of Europe. Why? Probably because we think that it carries more status to remain independent and separate.) But it's more subtle than the hackneyed idea that big is beautiful (Americans, like everyone else, don't consider beerguts and Big Macs to be particularly big status symbols.)

America is such a vast and diverse country, that status within it varies tremendously, far more than between Northern and Southern England, Scotland, Ireland and Wales. America is a comparatively young country compared to Europe so it derives less status from heritage and history. (Only recently, for example, was it of any status at all to have Native American blood in your veins.) That said, status is still an exceedingly important concept to Americans. For most people, money is status and status is money. The more of one, the more of the other.

But times are achanging. As Northern Europe becomes progressively more obsessed with money and material things, so too has America become a little less so, with more emphasis on European culture and British heritage. Status, like fashion, never stays still.

The way it was
In the last century you could have been a rich railroad tycoon, a cattle baron or simply the fastest gun in the west. You could have been one of the few who struck it rich in the Gold Rush. Your only means test might have been whose side you fought on in the Civil War, who you rode with (was it the Hole in the Wall Gang or the James/Younger Gang?), whether you were a frontiers man with scalps to boost your status among the redskins, or a peaceable card sharper stranded on the Mississippi with only Jack Daniels and a trusty Derringer for company.

Any of these roles could have given you status. Perhaps your ancestors came over on the *Mayflower*. Perhaps your godfather was a Godfather, or a Public Enemy No. 1. Perhaps they chose to fight on the side of the law with Eliot Ness or the Earps?

More relevant to the present day is how your family made its money. So long as it was in anything other than vice or real estate you're probably in the clear. Though of the two, vice is probably more forgivable.

The passing of the playboy

Americans along with the rest of the world (with the possible exception of the French) are firmly in agreement over one thing: that the playboy and his smooth satin sheets have finally disappeared down the waste disposal. Where once it was the ultimate dream to be a Hugh Hefner in a smoking jacket with your own private army of pneumatic bimbettes continually on tap, or one of the earlier playboy incarnations of Valentino, Novarro and Errol Flynn with their wild and wicked ways, nowadays the image has turned stale.

Perhaps it was George Hamilton who finally ruined the Playboy's image after he appeared in an Imelda Marcos home movie, singing 'Hello, Dolly/Imelda' on her birthday. As we cringed behind the sofa in embarrassment we thought 'Playboy Millionaire' Bruce Wayne could never have done such a thing, no, sir.

Feminism, the women's movement and the current antipromiscuity backlash have certainly contributed to his downfall. But possibly the final nail in the playboy's coffin stems from the fact that Americans prefer to work for their living these days, and hard too. The work ethic has simply replaced the leisure one. Perhaps people just got pissed off with satin sheets and generally acting like complete assholes. Whichever way you look at it, being a playboy doesn't constitute any kind of status any more.

Lawyers

Never admit to being a lawyer, especially in Washington. There are too many of them. They're everywhere. At cocktail parties, lawyers lie and tell people they work for the CIA or in public lavatories rather than admit the grim truth. Lawyer jokes abound, for example, 'What's the difference between a dead lawyer in the road and a dead skunk?' Answer: 'There are skid marks in front of the skunk.' And: 'How come Washington got all the lawyers and San Francisco all the gays?' Answer: 'San Francisco had first choice.'

Exit several other dearly held status symbols
The private limo
The Polo Lounge at the Beverly Hills Hotel
The Ku Klux Klan
Being director of the CIA
A Network party (especially on Tuesday afternoon)
Waterbeds and jacuzzis
White flared disco suits
Gold medallions
Lodges (except in *The Flintstones*)
Chivas Regal
Mountains of coke
The bikini
The Hollywood Bratpack

So what is status nowadays?
Any American is eligible to have and to hold status provided they are not a regular wearer of sneakers. Sneakers have become an emblem of non-status. Provided you are not a regular wearer of sneakers (once a week is allowable for casual wear, and they're OK to play sports in), many examples and manifestations of status will be the same as their European counterparts with the odd cultural difference.

Some examples of current US status
To be wealthy via anything but real estate
To be a yuppie who survived the crash
To be a pioneer in a gentrification area
To own two properties
To be able to park in Manhattan
To write, direct, produce and star in your own picture
To own a gallery or fashionable bookstore
To be a billionaire
To be a Vietnam Vet
To be a crime-busting public prosecutor

Any of these will do. But top of the list, yes, top of the list despite everything, it's probably the ultimate in US status to be . . . yup . . . a celebrity.

The celebrity

Whether you're Ray Krebs or Rhoda Morgenstern (for that matter whether you're Ray Krebs' nephew twice removed or Rhoda Morgenstern's niece by a previous incarnation), your status as a celebrity is sufficient for you to advertise cosmetics, do TV commercials, open supermarkets and host your own chat show.

To be a celebrity in America is to be a god. A king among mortals. A vegi-banger in a sausage factory. People will mob you in the streets. People will pretend to be the fathers and mothers of your children. People will assassinate you, and then turn you into a saint. It is not important what you are actually celebrated for. To be a celebrity is enough: 'And now, on tonight's show, will you please welcome our special guest star Alvie Nussbaum, former Idaho shoe salesman and former star of the sixties comedy series *Lemmings Island* which was taken off the air after only two disastrous episodes. Today Alvie makes coffee and sandwiches for Jimmy Carter's Presidential Comeback Campaign team. Ladies and Gentlemen, Mr Aaaaaalvie Nussbaum!'

Sports stars are probably the tops in the status stakes, followed by movie and TV stars, and billionaires. Politicians are quite low down, except for former Nixon/Watergate advisers turned good guys, e.g. G. Gordon Liddy.

Titles

In America there are titles for everything. If one doesn't exist, it will be invented. The Federal Government itself divides employees into eighteen grades, from Messenger to High Level Administrator. Such is the obsessive desire for status, that even dull and downmarket jobs have fancy titles, for example window cleaners have been known to be described as Transparent Wall Maintenance Engineers.

Since there are no hereditary ranks or titles, no honours to confer, and only a few top-hole regiments and smart clubs, Americans depend for snobbery, to a large extent, on their college and university hierarchy, and even the Ivy League has lowered its standards in recent years.

The upsurge of English and European influence
The result of a lack of hereditary ranks and titles has been that many class-conscious Americans have fallen back on Britain and certain other European countries as their class role model. There has been a surge of interest in imported class indicators such as regimental ties, Savile Row tailoring, suitable tartans and overall green welly culture. Hunting, shooting and fishing is only done with the snazziest equipment, whether four-legged or double-barrelled. Tea is beginning to replace cocktails. And a Range Rover isn't a bad automobile to have parked in your weekend home driveway.

American fashion designers, such as Ralph Lauren, have already spotted the trend and are even selling it back to its original creators at vastly inflated prices. Sylvester Stallone too has had some society/country culture injected into his pumped-up veins by East Coast superdeb Cornelia Guest.

The almighty dollar
Two American status mottos:
1. 'Rich is better than poor.'
2. 'Old money is preferable to new money.'
It's no status whatsoever to be poor in the US. Artists don't struggle, and no one suffers for their Art. 'Buddy, can you spare a dime' is an embarrassment and rags to riches stories are the favourite kind. The movie *Trading Places* was a fascinating piece of social comment because while a black person came to realize the American dream, two elderly whites were subsequently destroyed by it. White audiences laughed, but they laughed nervously.

Where to find old money
Palm Beach. The Hamptons on Long Island. Haddam in Connecticut. Bar Harbour in Maine. Newport on Rhode Island. And among the old established families: Rockefeller, Carnegie, Vanderbilt, Morgan, Rothschild, Stanford.

Old money tends to scorn workaday America, and particularly

the capital, despite all those embassy parties. Old money reads the *Washington Post* (an even greyer version of the *Daily Telegraph*) and keeps itself to itself. Outsiders, no matter how wealthy, are not at all welcome.

Education
Whereas the status of a British education hangs on what school you attended (public or otherwise), in America which college you went to is far more important. In Britain, though Oxford and Cambridge educations are preferred for some professions, so long as you have a brilliant degree from another university many employers will accept you all the same. Some US colleges that are renowned internationally are Yale, Harvard, Princeton, Stanford, Chicago and Berkeley, California. But, particularly in the area of business, colleges go in and out of fashion reasonably frequently.

College Status in America
Johns Hopkins (Maryland): medicine
Harvard (Massachusetts): law, business, political sciences – J.F.K. and Dukakis went there
Yale (Connecticut): political science – Bush went there
Princeton (New Jersey): law, business, political science – people going into Government go here
MIT (Massachusetts): engineering
Dartmouth (New Hampshire): law
Cornell (New York): hotel management
Syracuse (New York): journalism, advertising
UCLA (California): film
Stanford (California): medicine
Notre Dame (Indiana): football
Duke (North Carolina): law
Tulane (New Orleans): partying

SOME EAST AND WEST COAST DIFFERENCES

East Coast	*West Coast*
Belonging to a gym	Having a gym in your home

East Coast	West Coast
Getting into restaurants to eat	Getting into restaurants to be seen
Suntan 50 per cent of the time	All-year suntan, all over
Travelling around by cab in New York (cars are useless)	Travelling around by customized car or Range Rover
Going out, eating out. (There's no space in the apartment. The fridge is full of shoes)	'We can go out or stay in. Have some wine and cheese, and mellow out. We're pretty relaxed about the whole thing.'
Getting married in Europe	Getting married again in Las Vegas
Clothes for work: expensive designer wear Clothes casual: yuppie but different if possible	Active designer wear. Sweats and a Rolex. Looking healthy and rich
Yacht club	Yacht club
First home: A brownstone, for example the Dakota Building Second home: Upstate New York with some land	Beverly Hills next to a celebrity with pool, tennis court and maid. A movie star home kept the way it was Who needs a second home with a joint like this?
Set: the Art crowd. The Greenwich Village crowd. The Park Avenue crowd	Set: the Movie crowd. The rich Bratpack crowd
Art: owning a gallery in the Village	Art: 'Er, the cover of the new Van Halen album?'
The place: Manhattan with some space. Air space. Parking space. Anything	The place: 'Malibu, I guess. Near the beach. Somewhere where I can show off my pecs.'
Lifestyle: High-octane, cardiovascular, workaholic energy	Lifestyle: laid back
Sport: Racquet Ball	Sport: Hang-gliding on coke

Three big united status institutions
Women's Wear Daily terrorizes the fashion industry on both sides
of the Atlantic and regularly updates all that is in or out, clothing
and otherwise (NB: the short-lived English version has recently
ceased to be. Maybe the terrorism didn't appeal). *WW*'s boss is
one John Fairchild, sacred monster of the fashion world and
manipulator of Manhattan's social scene. He defines who and
what has fashionable status. The golden rule is that, though your
achievements are great, you as an individual must remain invisible. That is to say, the public will be well aware of your status
and standing without your having to sell or flaunt it *in front of
them*. Your status will be devalued, forfeit even, if you constantly
engage in ostentatious parties, pose for the paparazzi, allow your
homes to be photographed and displayed in *Interiors* and *House
and Garden* and, worst of all, pose for the press in the act of
passing over a generous charity cheque for some worthy cause
(for example Nicaraguan Contras, Battered Boyfriends) in finest
haute couture bought especially for the occasion, and costing
twelve times as much as the cheque you're handing over.

Fairchild himself ridicules limo culture, preferring to take the
subway to work, and has his own status all quite neatly defined,
with his 'invisible' circle of friends, his English wife, his Brooks
Brothers attire, his skiing parties at Klosters, and a seventeenth-
century farmhouse in Provence. The only criticism that is
occasionally levelled against ole J.F. is that he'll turn people into
celebrities and then turn on them for seeking publicity.

THE AMERICAS CUP: Since the Australians, backed by Alan Bond,
got their xxxxing hands on the Americas Cup in 1983, it has
turned into an international battle of power and money, waged by
syndicates that employ the very best sailors in the world to
compete in their extremely expensive state-of-the-art racing
yachts. (Bond is reputed to have spent about $110 million on his
last defence campaign.)

The race, no matter much money is involved, is the ultimate
status sporting event and only the very rich may apply, though
many, like Peter de Savary, are unsuccessful. Legal wranglings
pertaining to the date and place of the next race are achieving the
same status as the biggest criminal court proceedings. The last

race brought the Cup back to America, through the San Diego Yacht Club's victory, but the decision was later reversed in favour of New Zealand. The issue remains unresolved.

THE HAMPTONS: The Hamptons are America's East Coast seaside playground for the well-heeled and the well-keeled. They have become popular among those jaded by Malibu and Monte Carlo. A two-and-a-half-hour crawl up the Long Island Expressway or a forty-five-minute hop from La Guardia, the Hamptons appeal to those workaholics anxious to keep in contact with their Manhattan power bases while enjoying an apparently endless summer.

A decent house in the Hamptons might cost about $10 million. One worth writing to Jack and Angelica about, more like $10 million. The destination of an increasingly international crowd, the official Hamptons' season runs from Memorial Day Weekend (the last weekend in May) to Labour Day (the first Monday in September).

The Hamptons are a perpetual house party. You have to own a home, or be such essential company that you are a regular house guest. Operating from a hotel is bad news and forfeits several status points. Each Hamptons village has a different character.

SOUTHAMPTON: Society with a cap S. The crowd that winters in Palm Beach (the Gerald Fords and their guests and the near legendary Donald Trump).

EAST HAMPTON AND BRIDGEHAMPTON: The theatre and arts set – Alan Alda, Lauren Bacall, Eli Wallach, Christie Brinkley and Billy Joel, Calvin and Kelly Klein.

WEST HAMPTON: More the standard moneyed professions – doctors, lawyers, stockbrokers. Overall, house rental is very expensive, $50 Gs a month. $80 Gs for the whole season.

To crash a party on the Hamptons, a good ploy is to buy a ticket for one of the myriad charity events that define the season, for example the Parish Arts Museum and the Southampton Hospital. The cost of the ticket might be between $100 and $500.

Palm Beach

Palm Beach is that place in the movies where the rich fortune-hunters come to marry shy but sensitive money. Palm Beach is heavy status, all right. Most Americans would agree (especially those who live there). But it's so exclusive, such a bastion of inverted snobbery (the locals are up in arms since the Trumps set up camp there), that many Americans will simply bypass it as a status avenue, preferring alternative regal habitats such as Rhode Island.

No real British equivalent to Palm Beach exists, though aspects of it may be found among the Cotswolds or the Henley fraternity. To the uninformed, Palm Beach is a cigarette of land just off the southeast coast of Florida which is connected to the mainland by three bridges. The bridges open up to allow taller boats passage through Lake Worth. It is rumoured that they are also drawn up if there is trouble over in West Palm Beach, an area of high unemployment, a sort of Toxteth next to Belgravia.

Palm Beach is a community with rigid social stratifications. Palm Beach society is like a pyramid with a few very quiet, conservative individuals and families who have been around for many years at the top, who exert enormous influence on the community and those invited in or refused admission. These rarefied folk are rarely seen. They are not impressed by novelty, newcomers are regarded with suspicion, and new money with contempt.

THE RIGHT KIND OF PALM BEACH STATUS: Old Palm Beach: families like the Munns, the Drexells, the Biddels, whose WASP credentials are beyond reproach. They winter in Palm Beach, summer in Newport or the Hamptons. Their money is old enough to buy them the right to confer social recognition or to withhold it.

THE WRONG KIND OF PALM BEACH STATUS: 'Café People': those who buy second-mortgage tickets to charity balls. Those who grace the social pages of the Palm Beach *Daily News*, but don't get to be members of the essential clubs.

THE ESSENTIAL CLUBS: There are a number of Country Clubs to join in Palm Beach, but the most exclusive ones (simply referred to as 'the clubs') are the B&T (Bath and Tennis Club), membership around $25,000, and the Everglades Golf Club. Entry is restricted and postulants vetted to the nth degree. The question of who is and who is not a member is a subject of ceaseless fascination (especially to members). Breeding is the most important criterion. Rejection of B&T membership is social death.

Some big European status institutions

Cannes Film Festival

Cannes has ambivalent status. Some actors, directors and producers don't mind being seen at Cannes, while some mind a lot, and make a habit of giving it as wide a berth as possible. All advertising people go if they can, whether it's considered status or not. Most of them would sell their souls for a freebee. In all some 40,000 people attend.

The trick at Cannes is to be seen in the 'right' places, mix with the 'right' people and avoid (if possible) embarrassing encounters. These include being photographed with large-chested starlets of no fixed cinematic future, or making deals with obscure Mexican and Hungarian film producers who are certain to sink your film career as soon as it's begun. (Hungarian interpreter: 'Mr Tortilla sees this film as a kind of futuristic *Solomon and Sheba* which takes place at a Connie Francis/Pat Boone beach party. You'll be playing the beach hunk who rescues Sheba from the Werewolf.')

If you're not in the film business, Cannes can be great fun as well as a poseurs' paradise, and there are plenty of parties and receptions where many of the 'right' people may be found to interact meaningfully with. When not having fun or posing (Barry Normanspeak cuts in here), you might find yourself making deals, or at least pretending to make deals, in hotel lobbies (especially the Majestic). Ditto on as many hotel terraces as you can find (especially the Carlton). You might also find it good for your image to take a daily promenade along La Croisette. But whatever you do, don't sunbathe or take too many clothes off during the day, or you'll appear too relaxed to be making any kinds of deal, pretend or otherwise.

The more exclusive parties you go to, invited or gatecrash, the better, particularly if one's host is Maurice Tinchant at his villa in the hills. Finally, it's not a bad idea to catch up on some new films, since it always goes down well back home if you can say, 'The new Spielberg? Yeah, I caught it in Cannes.'

Monaco Grand Prix

The most social Grand Prix on the circuit, the race and track takes over the whole town. The Grimaldis (Prince Rainier and family) watch over the proceedings, supported by a whole glittering support cast of film and pop stars, socialites and well-heeled flotsam and jetsam. The Hôtel de Paris is the place to stay and the place to celebrate after the race. The pits is the place to watch the race, where naturally it helps to be on friendly terms with a driver or two. Currently the best team to be affiliated to is Alain Prost's Marlboro Team, but that could easily have changed by the time you read this.

While you're in Monaco, you may as well build up your status points even further with a trip to Monte Carlo and a spot of casino culture. The Monte Carlo Casino is probably the best casino in the world and host to the most glamorous of gamblers. It's heady *belle époque* atmosphere swiftly goes to your head as you day-dream yourself into an open-top white Jaguar XK150 S, with a Grace Kelly lookalike resplendent in sunglasses and a Hermès scarf by your side. A pride of smart greatcoated doormen and bellhops fight for the privilege of opening the car door for you and your lissom companion, who, once inside, slips away to powder her nose as you try your luck at the tables . . . The elegant crowd closes in. The conversational buzz is reduced to a whisper. The wheel spins. You make six consecutive bets on zero. You break the bank. As the millionaire's yacht pulls out of the harbour you suddenly notice you're not on it. Instead you awake with a start to find yourself clutching your last five-Franc chip, the croupier looking very bored in your direction as he asks, 'Any more bets, please?'

The Bayreuth Festival

The best music festival in the world. In Bayreuth's first year (1876) Mahler, Saint-Saëns, Liszt, Tchaikovsky and Grieg were among the audience. Liking Wagner is essential (the festival is, after all, still run by the Wagner family) but even that is an easy task compared to the difficulty of obtaining tickets. Tickets are booked years in advance and any powerful connections, no matter how remote, are mercilessly blackmailed by aficionados for a hint of influence in obtaining them.

The atmosphere at Bayreuth is highly stuffy and highly snobbish. At concerts and parties you may as well be stark naked on a zebra, some of the looks you're likely to receive. Yet being made to feel like a klutz is a small price to pay for the prestige of attending the festival. After all, 'You can go to Salzburg and see social-climbing German industrialists, you can go to Glyndebourne and see flashy British social climbers, but for pure absolute excellence in music you have to suffer at Bayreuth!' (Thomas Hoving).

Glyndebourne

'Flashy British social climbers.' Pah! What does he know? As far as many status point-scorers are concerned, Glyndebourne, in East Sussex, still heads the cultural calendar in Britain. In its Elizabethan country estate setting, traditional flavour (stiff upper lips and evening dress on the picnic lawn) and exceptionally high standard of opera (Sir Peter Hall is the Artistic Director, the London Philharmonic is the resident orchestra and top artists are drawn from all over the world), Glyndebourne is as English as a Spitfire fighter flying over a cornfield in World War Two. The whole event is incredibly exclusive, which is a key status requirement. The only way to guarantee tickets is to be or know a member of the festival society.

Small in scale and perfect in essence, only five or six operas are presented. The fact that you have to travel fifty miles out of London and dress up to the nines for a picnic in all weathers makes it all the more worthwhile. Status tips are to arrive reasonably early (well before the 5 P.M. start) and grab a good spot in the garden for the interval picnic. NB: rugs are the thing, rather than tables. Go completely over the top on the food and the wine since they are the only visible status symbols that can be compared given that everyone's dress follows the same code.

An exclusive international institution: The Tina Chow Set

Tina Chow is the fashion world's answer to the Scarlet Pimpernel. They seek her here, they seek her there, the good old paparazzi seek her everywhere. Married to international restaurateur Michael Chow (of Mr Chow), she slips in and out of the couture capitals meeting up with and bidding adieu to her international jet set of rich and dazzling friends, until of course they meet again. Because she travels so much, she gives the impression of being in several places at once.

The calling cry for this exclusive set is a discreet late-night transatlantic phone call to announce, 'I'll be in town Tuesday,' or, 'I'm flying out Saturday.' Such is the demand on the precious time of all the set members this is no idle threat. Get stuck in traffic on the way to J.F.K., and you might find this particular bird has flown.

Twice a year Tina swoops into London, and her arrival is preceded by a flurry of activity and excitement. The same fraught activity repeats itself in New York, Paris, and Tokyo. At most of the cool spots the couple touch down in and around the world, there is usually a Mr Chow restaurant, so the venues for the gatherings or 'meets' are usually *pas de problème*.

Fashion and being fashionable are the themes that underpin this set, and Tina herself has long been a fixture on the 'best-dressed' lists. Her role is one of fashion courier, relaying a nuance from Kyoto to Manhattan, cross-pollinating from Bond Street to the Avenue Marceau. No one can say if she's ever done anything really useful or proper, but that doesn't alter the fact that everyone still wants in.

The set members are a floating potpouri of glitterati and include Karl Lagerfeld, Jack Nicholson, David Bailey, Linda Evans, Linda Ronstadt, Christie Brinkley, Kenzo, Paloma Picasso, Rifat Ozbek, Michael Roberts, Manolo Blahnik, Rodney Kinsman,

Helmut Newton, Mick and Jerry, odd Durans and Iman. Andy
(Warhol) is sadly missed. John Walsh (whizz-kid *Sunday Times*
Literary Editor) recently had his application turned down. Reason
given? He wears a brown suit. Real reason? His rival international
set based at London's Groucho Club.

STATUS SYMBOLS

'He who dies with the most toys, wins' (US car sticker). A Rolex watch. Pah. A flying lady. Yawn. A Filofax and Mont Blanc *Meisterstück* pen, do me a favour. A jacuzzi. Zzzzz. These days status symbols go out of fashion quicker than almost everything else in the status world. Bang – there go Sony Walkmans. Bang – there go Rayban sunglasses and credit cards. There goes that posey silver-plated saxophone you still can't play. There go satellite dishes and one hasn't had a chance to experience them yet.

A classy status symbol used to be something rich and obvious like a diamond as big as the Ritz, or a sable coat or a chauffeur-driven Bentley. Each of these gave the holder a kind of instant unequivocal status. You couldn't argue with them, and as sought-after symbols they lasted quite a long time, indeed far longer than most of their modern counterparts. Though they are all a bit passé now, at the time they were easy to deal with.

Nowadays, the whole essence of status symbols has become a lot more complicated. With everybody having such easy access to designer labels, and the money to buy them, it's very hard to find a status symbol that sits still long enough to confer any real and lasting status on its owner. There is a demand now for the ugly, the banal and the tacky, for example Sid Vicious's last syringe, Des O'Connor's *Greatest Hits* (only three copies are known to exist, two of which are in maximum security bank vaults, not because of their value but because if they fell into the wrong hands they might be played in public).

Some status symbol guidelines

The first point to remember is that people can be the most valuable status symbols of all. You walk into a room with Isabelle

Adjani or Amanda Pays, or with William Hurt or Cyril Dodds in tow, and you won't need to wear your flashing-lights attention-demanding Lotus-Cortina Owners Club badge on your crotch. Secondly, it's important not to have too many status symbols. A few very high-powered ones will count for a lot more than a whole clutch of smaller ones.

Thirdly, when it comes right down to it, labels are just labels. For a label to be classed as a status symbol it must have some inherent value or worth. If a Chanel garment is a better-made, more exclusive garment than a C&A one, well and good. If it doesn't fit you or flatter you, it's not worth bragging about: 'I don't care if the label does say St Laurent, my darling, it still makes you look like Jabba the Hut.' Similarly, the most famous label in the world – Coca Cola – means very little in the West, but in rural China it's a rare and blatant capitalist symbol and anyone flashing a can bearing its name will be taken seriously.

Fourthly, and most importantly, the wrong kind of status symbols can forfeit all the status you've ever accumulated. We all shudder as we remember the incredibly expensive whale-foreskin bar stools on Onassis's luxury yacht, which were installed primarily to upset his female guests – 'Guess what you're sitting on, Miss Extremely-Refined Princess?'

Some current status symbols
- A Stradivarius violin (a perennial favourite)
- Your own private island
- La Perla underwear
- A helicopter (just)
- A collection of first edition P.G. Wodehouse.
- A knighthood (just)
- An Olympic Silver Medal (with all the drug tests you're more likely to get the Gold later)
- First night tickets
- Anything with the name Bugatti on it (cars, furniture, etc.)
- A three-star Michelin rating (for restaurants, not car tyres)
- Your own airline (formerly the main contender was Freddy Laker, now it's Richard Branson)
- A lil' ole Arl Well (translation: several large oil wells)
- A signed copy of *The Complete Cool Handbook*

- Davidoff Cigars
- A harem
- A dedication in a Graham Greene novel
- A Ferrari Boxer BB 512 (scarce Ferrari, 1976–81. Value soaring. Anywhere between a quarter and half a million pounds).
- A full-sized snooker table and a room to put it in
- A yacht longer than Donald Trump's (over 280ft)
- A sensory deprivation tank
- A racehorse that wins the Grand National
- A painting by Max Ernst
- The new *Oxford English Dictionary* (20 volumes/5,000 new words). You don't need it but you can tell everyone you paid £1,500 for it
- A Hasselblad camera
- A Purdey shotgun
- A Harley Davidson motorcycle
- A kidney donor card
- Fresh cut flowers in your home every day
- Fresh air

Some status materials
- Cashmere (says more about you than mere cash)
- Emeralds (takes fractionally longer to say than 'diamonds')
- Plutonium
- Walnut
- Platinum (similar to plutonium, but may attract slightly fewer bearded admirers and rather more of the female variety)
- Silk (a very refined fabric, implies its owner is sensitive and, paradoxically, a sexually intimate person as well as slightly chaste) NB: For men, silk ties rather than shirts
- Lace (a complex fabric, implies its owner is highly artistic as well as completely raunchy)
- Rubies (implies heirlooms and rich ancestry)
- Wool (cool and sophisticated)

Symbols that clash
Many of the following, though symbols of high status in their day, have now become debased through overuse and over-exposure.

Where once they evoked gasps of wonder and amazement, now the gasps are more of 'I wonder why?' as in 'I wonder why they bother?' and amazement as in 'It amazes me that people can be so vulgar.'

- Customized Rolls-Royces (personalized number plates, gold flying ladies, buffalo-hide seats)
- Caviar
- Mink coats
- Watches (not wearing a watch is a sign of status. It implies you, have plenty of free time – a valuable status commodity)
- Three-piece suits (even if you are aware that gentlemen don't close the last button of the waistcoat)
- A graphic equalizer (everyone a recording engineer in the comfort of their own living room – 'I think we need a touch more middle eight, third cymbal there, don't you? It sounds ever so as if Barry Manilow's actually in the room, don't you think?')
- Tattoos (even pretty little hummingbird ones on perfectly shaped buttocks aren't status)
- Cellular car phones (the Alex cartoon strip jokes in the *Independent* are starting to wear a bit thin)
- Things made of ivory (even worse than furs, not only are they cruel, they give their owners a souvenir shop image, even if they were bought in Nairobi)
- Aphrodisiacs and other sexual stimulants (for example powdered bat saliva, spanish fly, stud sprays)
- Anything with the name Porsche on it (except toilet paper)
- Monogrammed shirts and other personalized items (status people don't have to stake a claim on what is obviously theirs in the first place)
- Gold chains ('I bought my boyfriend one from Ratner's for Valentine's Day.' 'I bought my girlfriend one from Ratner's on Valentine's Day.' Together: 'Ever so cheap')
- Credit cards
- Too much black ('Everything in my home, even the flowers, are black')
- Air conditioning (too clinical. Too many CFCs)
- Silver coke spoons

- A bank overdraft (nothing big or butch about this any more)
- Garden gnomes
- Mirrors on the ceiling (the Bitch/Stud image of the seventies has about as much status as a *Carry On* film without Sid James)
- Uzi machine guns (the ones that all the trendy drug dealers carry)

Non-status materials
- 100 per cent polyester ('Amazin'. You don't need to iron it!')
- Nylon ('Even more amazin' than polyester. Or is it the other way round? Though I must admit, the sweat stains are a bit difficult to get out. Are yours yellow too?')
- Denim (especially with splits in the knees)
- Plastic
- Pine
- Gold
- Leather (except for shoes – a leather jacket is now the commonest article of clothing in the Western hemisphere)

Pets as status symbols

The Queen has her corgis. David Bailey has his parrots. James Hunt has his budgies. The Sultan of Aqaba his pet tigers. But are we really that impressed? Pets as status symbols go in and out of fashion with alarming regularity. The trend seems to be going away from the tradition of dogs, cats, birds and white mice towards the more rare, exotic and wild creatures of the world; especially if they turn out to be very slimy and more than a bit on the disgusting side. In terms of domestic pets, pedigree still counts for status and a dog who wins a category at Cruft's is still big biz.

On the wild side, if you can keep the animal in surroundings as close to its natural environment as possible, then you're getting pretty close to pet status. Overall, the emphasis seems to be on the wild, the dangerous and the intelligent.

STATUS PETS: Watery creatures are big status at the moment. We'd all love an otter, a seal, a dolphin or a killer whale even though we accept that they shouldn't be taken out of their natural environment. Bats, slugs and spiders are increasingly 'in' as status pets, as are snakes. Meerkats, racoons and skunks are also in at the moment, as a reaction against domestic felines, but it means you'll have to change your habitat fairly radically. Trained hawks and kestrels are the birds to have. And racing pigeons are no longer the working class property they once were.

NON-STATUS PETS: Dogs that look like their owners. Barbara Cartland-type lap-yap dogs, pit bull terriers, Dobermans, Alsatians. (The most status dog you can have is a working sheep dog.) Fat, over-pampered flea-bitten cats. The only cats to have are the ones with *Top Cat* streetwise attitudes.

Horses are out, replaced in the status pet stakes by ordinary old donkeys and Shetland ponies who are never likely to win the Grand National.

NB: A pack of savage guard dogs, piranhas or sharks in the grounds of your home is an indication of something valuable to be protected, human life as well as a private property, but they have nothing to do with pet status.

Awards and gongs

In the West we're a very self-congratulatory type of people. When we've achieved something great or excelled ourselves we need to reward our efforts with visible and advertised acclamations, so we can feel special or elevated compared with lesser-achieving mortals. We must have something to show for our trouble – like medals and diplomas and prizes and scholarships and badges.

In primitive tribes similar acclamations do exist, but frequently these take the form of colourful scars on the body and face, rings and stretch objects in the lips, nose and ear.

Each to their own. Nevertheless awards and rewards are an accepted part of life's status. Invariably people go over the top with what seems to be an acceptable system. Nowadays there seem to be awards for more or less everything (for example typographical awards for the best use of space, the Denis Healey

Award for the most outstanding contribution to eyebrow forma-
tions) and the whole system is in danger of falling into disrepute.

In times of war each country has had its ultimate bravery
recognition (the Victoria Cross, the Knight's Cross, the Croix de
Guerre, the Silver Star, etc.). The status of these matched their
rarity, and they were often awarded posthumously. (Ever noticed
how many Kings, Queens and Heads of State have racks of medals
and crests on their chest but never went to within two continents
of a battlefield?)

Some top prizes for some professions

In literature it's the Booker Prize, the Whitbread Prize (UK) or
  the Nobel Prize for Literature (International).
In science it's a Nobel Prize or employment on the Star Wars
  programme. In journalism it's a Pulitzer prize.
In advertising it's a Gold Design and Art Direction Award. A
  BTAA (UK). A One Show (US). A Palme d'Or (International).
In the movies it's an Oscar for either Best Actor/Actress, Best
  Film, or Best Director (others like the best Latvian folk music
  score for a low budget film don't count).
In athletic sport it's an Olympic Gold, Silver or Bronze Medal.
In law it's your own TV series.
In medicine it's your own clinic or your own syndrome.
In politics it's your own way or your own 'ism': Thatcherism,
  Marxism.
In industry it's a Queen's Award, a Knighthood, or simply tons of
  mulah.

Titles and ranks

Titles and ranks are a fairly formal way of bestowing status. Along
with letters before and after a name, they tend to be the first form
of status you are aware of when first coming into contact with a
person. For example, having Your Highness, Lord, Lady, Dr,
General or Sir in front of your name will immediately give some
status information about you.

There are hierarchies in most professions and institutions, and
most of us will be completely familiar with many of the more
common ones. Managing Director and Archbishop we know carry

more status than the positions of Senior Clerk and Priest, but not as much as the positions of Chairman and Cardinal.

In Britain, titles of the aristocracy start at the top with the royal family, followed by Dukes, Marquises, Earls, Viscounts, Barons, Baronets, Knights, Squires, and plain old plebby commoners (i.e. the rest of us). 'Lord of the Manor' has a nice status ring about it until you discover that the Manor is opened to the public and that Lord and Lady take tea with pensioners in the Great Dining Hall to supplement their income.

In the Army, some regiments carry more status than others (Coldstream Guards, Household Cavalry, the Black Watch, the Queen's Own Highlanders, the Atholl Highlanders) and the SAS is highly regarded for its capabilities in extremely dangerous situations. By a strange quirk, the rank of Major, though a fairly superior position, carries very little status since it is considered to be a 'never quite made it to the top' rank.

The alternative title list
There are other titles, apart from the formal ones donated by society, that also carry status, sometimes a lot more than their traditional counterparts, particularly in the press.
The one and only
The infinitely unique
The near legendary
The legendary (even better than the 'near')
The extremely eligible
The reclusive
The unpredictable
The dynamic
The Symbol of the Age
The simply irresistible
Public Enemy No. 1
Wunderkind

TRANSPORTATION

The car

Remember when only the mega-rich drove Rolls-Royces and Bentleys and a Mark 2 Jaguar or an MGB represented the ultimate in sportiness? When people could distinguish the extra degrees of status between a Jaguar-looking-Daimler and a Jaguar-looking-Jaguar? Remember when every woman you knew was crazy 'bout automobiles, and the sooner you passed your test the better?

Remember when cars had large boots, and cruddy mileage per gallon didn't really seem that important when you were hammering down the third lane of the M1 with your foot to the ground and your speedo dangerously in the red zone? Remember when every other car wasn't a hatchback? Remember the days before traffic-jams, all-day rush hours and 120-mile motorway tailbacks?

Car status is rapidly on the wane because it's simply no longer any fun to drive. Sleek fast beasts with 16-valve turbocharged V12 engines sit in jams next to 2CVs. And BMW advertisements inform us that the true test of a performance car is how well it does in crawling along at 5 mph in traffic. Ever since a company car became a significant part of a job package in some sectors, everyone, it seems, drives a GTi, a BMW, a Mercedes or a Porsche. Consequently, their status has diminished.

RULE NO. 1 about car status is, if you have a status car (see below) it is best leave it parked all nice and gleaming in your driveway during the day. Travel to work by public transport or preferably by taxi during the week. And only take it out on Saturday night or on Sunday. More and more the status of cars is to do with how nice they look standing still rather than stuck in traffic.

RULE NO. 2: Having a personal chauffeur is still status, but travelling in rented limousines (particularly in the US) is not.

RULE NO. 3: To have any of the following on your car demands immediate relegation to zero status:

Spoilers
Gold 'silver ladies' and quaint little silver horses or foxes
H. R. Owen stickers
A cellular car phone
Black or opaque windows
CD plaque (genuine)
Larger than life antennae
A turbo-charged engine

Status cars

FERRARI: Most Ferraris, especially Daytona (1968–73), GTO, Dino 246GT (1969–73), Boxer BB512 (1976–84), limited edition GTO (only 200 made).

MERCEDES: Pre-1970 Mercedes Coupés (particularly 280SE Coupé Convertible) and pre-1970 sports cars, particularly the distinctive-shaped Gullwing (1953–6).

ASTON MARTIN: DB5 (extra points for convertible), DB3S, DB4GT Zagato.

JAGUAR: E Type Jaguar Series 1 (3.8-litre) Roadster, D Type, XJ 220 (£336,000 if you're lucky). Jaguar XK 120 and 140 (to a lesser extent XK 150).

LAMBORGHINI: Miura (1966–9), preferably roadsters.

MASERATI: Bara (and any Maserati built between 1958 and 1980).

DE TOMASO: Pantera.

BRISTOL: Old ones only. Max Lubin in *Capital City* has one.

CITROËN: Light 15s. DS and DE.

NB: unlike Rolls-Royces, Bentleys still carry status (see below).

Non-status cars
The obvious (hatchbacks, Marinas, Fords)
Most BMWs (except 1957 507 Roadster and 1937–9 328 sports).
  The jury is still out on the limited edition 959
Porsches (except the 356C)
Many Rolls-Royces (except the 1914 alpine Rolls-Royce, 1962
  Rolls-Royce Silver Cloud II)
Most definitely not a Lamborgini Countach. The ultimate example
  of Stringfellowstatus (i.e. none)
Most Peugeot or Golf GTis (yuppie status isn't real status)
The Ferrari Testarossa is the wrong Ferrari unless it happens to
  be the 1957 version. The limited edition F40 only has status
  because of its price
Jeeps and 4x4s (excluding Land Rover) are more yuppie status (a
  Range Rover may just slip through the net)

Flying

Flying used to have a lot of status. Flying used to be very expensive
and therefore rather uncommon. Only Americans used to fly.
Everyone else travelled by boat or train. As flying became more
common, your status was determined by how far you were flying
and on what type of aircraft. It wasn't sufficient to fly to Guernsey
by Viscount. You had to go to the Far East by VC10.

Jet lag was the first sign of flying status. A whole lexicon of
heavy flight terminology came into being. People talked of catch-
ing the in-flight movie (which natch hadn't been released back
home yet). People talked of joining the Mile High Club, and
getting blitzed on free alcohol, which interfered with the 'ludes
you'd taken that morning, hence those bleary red eyes covered by
Raybans and the cool six o'clock shadow.

It all seems a little passé now. Like the bore who always likes
to point out that he's the last person to board the aircraft. It's all
a bit of a yawn. Nowadays it seems that flying status is centred

around the refreshed and raring-to-go type. The one who can't wait to get to that Apple Computer meeting in Manhattan. Plus there are no in-flight movies on private jets, so who needs to mention them?

On Concorde there is only one class, so forget the one-upmanship of bragging about flying first class.

Can you pilot a biplane? That's the sort of question you should be asking with regard to flight status. Do you own your own sea plane? Do you own your own airline? Forget about owning a paltry little Lear Jet – the one to have at the moment is either a new Falcon 900 tri-jet (room for twelve, cost $19 million), or a Gulfstream Aviation G3, like the Aga Khan's, which costs about $5,000 an hour to operate. Finally, are you booked on the Space Shuttle?

Trains

If you've travelled by train at all it's got to have been the Orient Express, preferably all the way to China rather than just to Venice. It's best to grab a trip on a steam locomotive before they're all phased out. Some of the best, and therefore most status, routes are in South Africa, for example the Banana Express (Port Shepstone to Izingolweni), the Apple Express (Port Elizabeth to Loerie), Tootsie (Mossel Bay to Knysna) and the Blue Train (South Africa's answer to the Orient Express). Beyond that, it's hardly something to brag about if you got the Wimbledon to Waterloo train, unless of course you managed to grab a seat by the window and no one threw up over you.

Boats

Forget liners of the *QE2* variety; if you want to cruise it's got to be in private yachts that sail the world and drop anchor in distant ports to pick up supplies and opulent guests whom you haven't seen in absolutely ages. Either that, or big powerful Florida-type fishing boats, with Marlin on the horizon being pulled this way and that by your Levi stitching, as you chew on your cigar end and swig out of a foaming beer can, before cutting the line and letting the noble fish go.

Motorcycles

Old English in mint condition (Nortons, Triumphs). And especially, Harley Davidsons. No Jap bikes whatsoever.

THE ARTS

At the moment, among the status arts are interior decoration, radio, and sculpture. The interior decoration is done by someone else and status names are usually tracked down in the upmarket *Interiors* magazines. Radio is both listening as well as broadcasting. Radio 4 is the status station. You can't get more trendy than *The Archers* nowadays. Meanwhile, in the world of the creative professions, everyone wants to have their own radio production company. Sculpture can be as amateurish as you like (you can always call your failed 'Wrestlers' 'Person with more limbs than most' or 'Tarantula fights off an attack of killer armadillos'). And so long as you have a big studio, a couple of tons of various materials, a headscarf and a clay-stained leather apron, no one will know whether you have any talent or not.

Architecture is at a bit of a low point status-wise, at present. Theatre is enjoying a boom. Perhaps it's the high ticket prices that are attracting people. Chekhov, the American classics (Eugene O'Neill, Tennessee Williams, Arthur Miller), anything with Alan Bennett and anything directed by Peter Brook or starring Sarah Crowden are the ones to see. Modern dance and classical ballet are also big status at the moment. Arts festivals are status generally. Polverigi in Italy. Madrid International Theatre festival. Mayfest in Glasgow. LIFT in London. Opera is the essential pastime of the status slave (q.v.), and everyone is working on one from David Byrne of Talking Heads to 'talking head' Jonathan Miller.

Status at the movies

FOR DIRECTORS: It's growing a beard like Francis Ford Coppola. Spending millions of dollars of someone else's money, making a disaster, and still being forgiven a couple of years later and given another chance. Being a director carries as much status as being a glamorous star, if not more.

FOR STARS: It's getting to sleep with a great many of the opposite sex. Winning an Oscar. Getting a pavement star outside Grauman's Chinese Theatre. Being invited to Swifty Lazar's party on Oscar night. And getting to do a nude scene with Beatrice Dalle in *Betty Blue*.

FOR THE PUBLIC: NFT membership is good. Your own private viewing theatre is better. Seeing films before Barry Norman is good. Having an opposing view to him is better. Knowing who all the key grips, gaffers and best boys are on each movie as well as the supporting actors and actresses and the second director. Being an extra in a film is fairly low status, but quite a hoot when it's only discovered after the film has been released that where there's a placard in a crowd scene that should read 'Workers of the World Unite', one instead reads 'Hello, Mum, it's me, Kevin.'

Status movies to have seen (or at least mention in cinema queues)
Abel Gance's *Napoleon*
Sergei Eisenstein's *The Battleship Potemkin*
Sergei Eisenstein's *Ivan the Terrible*
Erich von Stroheim movies, especially *Greed*, *Queen Kelly*
Ingmar Bergman movies, especially *Wild Strawberries*
Jean Renoir's *Grand Illusion* (the key grip was Jean-Claude, the gaffer was Jean-Paul)
Jacques Rivette's *Celine and Julie Go Boating*
Federico Fellini's *La Dolce Vita*
Michael Cimino's *Heaven's Gate* (uncut version)
David Lean's *Lawrence of Arabia* (new complete version)
The new Russian cinema generally, with the possible exception of Tarkovsky films

The status of art

So-called art is everywhere. You just can't get away from it these days. There's arts programmes on the TV, there's an abundance of art around town. Every four seconds a new art gallery springs up in London (every 1.75 seconds in New York). Every sixteen seconds an exciting new artist is discovered in New York (18.76 seconds in London).

Though it's all around us, there is no substitute for good paintings and sculpture, and they still represent one of the important status symbols. If you're famous, and you've got plenty of spare cash, bung it into an art collection, Jonathan. Join Baron Heini Thyssen, Charlie Saatchi, Yves St Laurent, Karl Lagerfeld, the late Peggy Guggenheim and a host of others. Start off with a small Picasso or Vuillard drawing and work your way up to a Van Gogh after the half-yearly results have come out.

It's a good time to be an artist these days, even one of dubious talent. Painters are far more likely to become a financial success in their own lifetime now than in any period previously recorded. Current painters to own are Julian Schnabel (US), Howard Hodgkin and Noel Coward. On the up are young Scottish artists, H. M. Bateman and Stanley Spencer. And remember one Egon Schiele or Gustav Klimt is worth at least a dozen David Hockneys.

- For full status, the collector must have his collection on display, and then preferably at home rather than in a gallery. It carries no status whatsoever to have your art collection locked away in a bank vault.

- As the status of art goes up, so does the status of owning a gallery. A gallery owner is a particularly status thing to be in New York.

- There can almost be too much art, or at least too much talk about art. There's a current boom in arts programmes and their presenters have been riding high in the status charts for the last fifteen years. But they could be about to take a dive status-wise with the current over-exposure, and the explosion in young, trendy, Channel 4-type arts programmes presented by Scots, by the masses for the masses. So if you're thinking about a career in arts presentation, it may be a good idea to set your sights on current affairs or investigative TV journalism, which are on the way up.

Instant ways to lose your status with art

- Over-analyse it: *Person A* (about to lose his status): 'Rothko manifests an abstract expressionism based on theological considerations that are typified by the fondness for monasticism and bombast that you see before you.' *Person B*: 'That's not a Rothko, that's a Jasper Johns.'

- Display complete ignorance, for example, praise the exquisite artistic features of a fire bucket or an exit door in a museum of modern art, in all seriousness and not as a joke.

- Buy a poor forgery that has already been authenticated by experts.

- Be the expert who authenticated the forged picture.

- Enthuse over really obscure artists (whom in reality you can't abide), while slagging off the traditional ones that you really like, for example Turner and Rembrandt, because they're 'untrendy'.

- Spending your money on limited edition prints made of papier-mâché and putting them in the reception area of your company.

- Owning more than eleven pictures with Celia Birtwell in them.

- Paying more than £15,000 for a Jackson Pollock. *An instant way to gain status with a Jackson Pollock?* You hang it upside down and nobody notices.

STATUS IN SPORT

With professional sports having such high status in the US, it's only a question of time before the same happens in Britain. In the meantime, however, professional sports and sportsmen do not quite have the celebrity status (and the big bucks) that they enjoy in the States. Over the pond, needless to say, sportsmen are quintessentially 'over the moon' about their revered status.

Whereas all the heavy physical stuff (football, boxing, ice hockey and to a lesser extent baseball) carries higher status in America (as Frank Bruno found out recently to his advantage), in England it is the more refined games rather than the physical sports that tend to carry the status for example tennis, cricket, rowing, horsey stuff.

It is also true that once a sport has suffered from over-exposure, once it has got its own Channel 4 TV series, the time has come to steer clear. And if Emlyn Hughes or Bill Beaumont can answer a question about it correctly on *A Question of Sport* it's unlikely that it has much credibility any more.

SOCCER: Though soccer is our national game, recent events on the terraces have brought it into disrepute. Liverpool FC is the team in Britain that has the most status (Football League champions three times in a row, '81, '82, '83; four times European Champions, '76, '77, '80, '83; four times Littlewoods Challenge Cup winners, '80, '81, '82, '83; FA Cup winners, '73, '85). Nottingham Forest also have status owing to their charismatic leader Brian Clough.

RUGBY: Of the two types of rugby, Rugby League, though a professional sport, carries far less status than Union, which is amateur. Playing for the national side and being in any team that beats the French is high status indeed.

ATHLETICS: Athletics really only comes into its stride round the time of the Olympics, but then its status goes through the roof. Breaking records, particularly world records, particularly for short sprinting races (100, 200, 400 metres) is mega-status, provided you beat the dope test afterwards.

PROFESSIONAL SNOOKER AND DARTS: Neither has much status, such is their over-exposure.

SKIING: Skiing for fun is still a big status sport which tends to be more valued in Europe than in the US. Professional skiers enjoy heavy status especially those involved in downhill racing and ski-jumping. Eddie Edwards, though a spunky sporting chap, continues to fail with alarming regularity. Contrary to the British habit of patting failures on the back, and the equivalent British failure to reward success, status is about the latter and the quicker everyone realizes it, the better. Having done the Cresta Run in St Moritz is indicative of skiing status. Being a member of the Gunther Sachs ultra-rich ultra-old-hat 'Dracula Club' is not.

BASEBALL (SPECTATING AS WELL AS PLAYING): Rapidly gaining status in Britain on the back of trendy softball. Learn about the big inning theory (note the singular – calling them 'innings' is a big giveaway) and how to read a box score. Drop phrases like 'sacrifice bunt', 'pinch hitter' and 'designated hitter'. Essential reading is Thomas Boswell's *How Life Imitates the World Series*. In the US, the team to follow is the Red Sox or Twins.

STATUS SPORTS TO WATCH
    County cricket, especially Worcestershire (but only the first day)
    Head of the River Race (but not the Varsity version)
    The Tour de France (be in Paris for the last day)
    Australian Rules football
    Women's ice hockey

Basketball in the US (Boston Celtics and the LA Lakers – the team all the stars follow)

Sumo wrestling

STATUS SPORTS TO PLAY
  Real tennis (not lawn)
  Ballooning
  Hovercraft racing
  Judo (not karate)
  Canoe polo
  White water raft racing
  Men only: lacrosse
  Women only: soccer
  Rugby League
  Ice hockey

STATUS INJURIES IN SPORT: Hamstring. Broken nose (especially for women). Broken leg. Never admit to a groin strain, however.

A STATUS PASTIME: Croquet.

Status games and sporting events

Polo
Status indeed. Royals do it. Lords and ladies do it. The International money set do it. Steve McQueen did it in *The Thomas Crown Affair*. Ralph Lauren has a fashion collection named after it. Cartier are big sponsors of it. The men all cut a dashing figure in their boots and togs. The women, if they're not playing, look absolutely spiffing on the polo lines, and have been known to shout out quite loudly in support, particularly if old 'Chukka' (Prince Charles) is about.

Anyone who can't afford the ponies and the upkeep, or hasn't quite got the right connection, can jolly well puck off. Arrival is by Jet Ranger helicopter or at the least in an Aston Martin Volante. Call Fergie's dad 'Major' not 'Ronnie' or there will be a bit of a stink. And finally beware of the dashing Argentinian contingent. Remember what happened to Fergie's mum!

A COUPLE OF DECENT POLO CLUBS: Guards Polo Club. President: the Duke of Edinburgh. Players: the Prince of Wales, Oliver Ellis, Julian Hipwood.

Royal County of Berkshire: Chairman: Bryan Morrison. Players: Lord Charles Beresford, Stephanie Powers (*Hart to Hart*), Howard Hipwood, Kenny Jones (ex-drummer with The Who).

OTHER PLAYERS: Stewart Copeland (ex-Policeman), Claire Tomlinson, Sammy Moreno, Lord Cowdray, Memo Gracida.

POLO STATUS EVENTS: Argentine Open (Palermo, Nov.Dec.), World Cup (Palm Beach, March), British Open (Cowdray Park, July), Gold Cup (Deauville, Aug.), Gold Cup (Sydney, Easter).

Racing

The sport of kings; nurtured and enjoyed for centuries by the British aristocracy, and the envy of the world. Nowadays it's an international event with Greeks, Arabs and Aussies all competing. Though the horses may cost millions, the horse fanciers are rarely in it to make money. Those who love the sport are obsessive in their enthusiasm. Meetings are open to everyone. But which entrance you go through is vital in determining your status. Royal Ascot requires vouchers for admission into the royal enclosure and the list for new applications has been closed until further notice. With a voucher for the royal enclosure, you can still get to the paddock and the Turf Club tent (members only), where all the smart people hang out (Hugo Kondratiuk, Louise Mitchell, Robert Sangster etc.).

The Derby also has a voucher system. If you have a runner that day, you are allowed two free badges per horse. Wives and daughters of Jockey Club members also get in free but have to sport a badge with their name. Arrival at the course, to maximize your status, should be by helicopter or Range Rover. Arrive before lunch, buy your race card, timeform, copies of *Sporting Life* and *Racing Post* and head for the nearest members' bar.

Dressing up is for Ascot and Derby days, and optional at Goodwood (Panama hats). For ordinary flat racing on a Monday afternoon at Leicester, you will be laughed off the course for

dressing up. But don't forget your 'bins'. Social chit-chat ceases as
a race starts and begins the moment it's over.

THE SEASON: The flat season runs from March to November, with
its high point in June, July and August. These meetings tend to
be pretty fashionable affairs, where the accepted attire is hats, silk
dresses, and morning suits.

The status set are seen at: The Newmarket Guineas in April
and May. The Epsom Derby, Oaks Meeting and Royal Ascot, in
June. The King George VI and Queen Elizabeth Stakes at Ascot
in July. Goodwood at the end of July. York in August. Ayr in
September. And Doncaster for the St Leger in September.
Important Jump Meetings: Cheltenham Mackeson Gold Cup in
November. Newbury Hennessy in November. Kempton on
Boxing Day. Cheltenham Festival in March. The Grand National
at Aintree in April.

Important Foreign Flat Meetings: The Kentucky Derby. The
Melbourne Cup. The Italian Derby in Rome. The Queen's Plate
Stakes, Canada. The Irish Guineas at the Curragh. The Budweiser
Irish Derby. The Phoenix Park Cartier Million. The August
Deauville meeting. Prix De L'Arc De Triomphe, Longchamps,
Paris.

BIG JUMP OWNERS: The Queen Mum, Basil Thwaites, Colonel
Whitbread, Mrs Christine Feathers, Anne, Duchess of Westminster, Mrs Miles Valentine, Jim Joel, Lord Vestey, Peter Hopkins.

BIG FLAT OWNERS: The Maktoum brothers, Stavros Niarchos, the
Queen, the Aga Khan, Robert Sangster, Lady Beaverbrook, Lord
Howard De Walden, Jim Joel (again), Louis Freedman, The
Marchioness of Tavistock, Sir Michael Sobell, Paul Mellon.

Sport: the best of the rest
Tennis: The All England Club Tennis Championships,
    Wimbledon
Motor racing: The Monaco Grand Prix, Monte Carlo
Sailing: The Americas Cup (see United Status). The Admiral's
    Cup, Cowes, England
Cricket: The Ashes, Lords. The Ashes, Sydney, Australia

Rowing: Henley Royal Regatta, Oxfordshire. Lucerne Regatta, Switzerland

River fishing: Salmon – Scotland: the Spey, Tweed, Tay, Dee. Trout – England: the Test, the Itchen

Pacific salmon fishing: Alaska: Bristol Bay

Lake fishing, Canada: Huntsville, Ontario

Golf: best courses are Royal and Ancient, Scotland; Cypress Point Club, California; Quinta Do Lago, Algarve, Portugal

Fox hunting: still high status in upper-class circles despite the controversy (NB: the Shrewsbury Hunt Club doesn't hunt).

Shooting: best moors are Abbeystead, Lancashire; Dallowgill, Yorkshire.

Skiing: best resorts are St Moritz, Gstaad, Zermatt, Klosters (Switzerland); Courcheval, Val D'Isère (France).

ANTI-SOCIAL BEHAVIOUR AND STATUS

Surviving a scandal

Everyone loves a scandal. We like to imagine what it feels like to be the centre of attention, the focus of public scrutiny, the object of derision as your private life is dragged across the front page of the tabloids accompanied by lurid out-of-focus photographs that are more likely to be Princess Stephanie and her latest toyboy than you.

Under any other circumstances we would welcome such valuable publicity. Agents would pay a Jonathan King's ransom for the privilege of so much free space to promote their stars. But not in the case of a slimy scandal that might damage irreparably a valuable reputation.

One might even get away with a mild scandal – 'Famous peer shouted at our dog' sensation; 'Rock star faithful to his wife' storm – but if it's going to be on the front page of the *Sun* you can be sure that they're out for blood.

Since the fate of those involved in a scandal is invariably loss of power, privilege, spouse and family, and general social leprosy, there is a great fascination for those individuals involved in such scandals. Though we are not necessarily against them, though we might even sympathize with them, we also find ourselves mentally rubbing our hands in glee, like spectators in a Roman arena watching. Christians v the Lions, as we are comforted by the consideration, 'There but for the grace of God, go I.'

The odds on surviving a scandal are very slim. Those who do survive are rare creatures indeed. If their reputation is restored or remains intact, we, who were originally ambivalent about their fate, instantly bestow on the survivors very high status indeed.

History is peppered with famous scandals

Antony and Cleopatra's love affair.

Richard III and the deaths of the Princes in the Tower.

King Alfred, who burnt the cakes and, though hardly a hanging offence even in that century, no one has let him forget it.

Henry VIII survived the scandal of having six wives by setting up his own church and making it all legal.

Oscar Wilde unfortunately did not survive the Lord Alfred Douglas trial.

Nelson survived the Lady Hamilton escapade by winning all his sea battles.

D. H. Lawrence survived *Lady Chatterley's Lover*.

Surviving a Scandal Rule No. 1

Not giving a damn about the consequences helps a person to survive a scandal, for example Wellington's 'Publish and be damned' challenge to his mistress.

Surviving a Scandal Rule No. 2:

It helps to be a Royal.

ROYALTY: Being a royal family member should be a position inspiring such infinite public loyalty that one would suppose it would be very difficult to survive a scandal in this job. Yet royals do have one very big advantage. Their arrangement with the press is such that there is a great deal of restraint when chronicling royal faux pas. Fergie's dad came off quite lightly in the recent massage parlour scandal, and once he had made his peace with the Queen and Charles, no more was spoken about it. Princess Margaret's breakup with Lord Snowdon was reported with relative restraint, as were Prince Andrew's flirtations with Koo Stark, the former actress. The scandal of the century was the abdication of Edward VIII and his subsequent marriage to Mrs Simpson, a divorcee. Yet, despite the apparent gravity of his actions, much of the country sympathized with the couple. It was even overlooked that Edward had been entertained by Adolf Hitler at the time. Will Prince Philip be forgiven for attending the funeral of the ex-Emperor of Japan, whom many consider to be a war criminal? It's more than likely.

POLITICS: Political scandals are big news, surviving them even bigger. The higher the position the greater the status of the survivor. John and Bobby Kennedy survived with their reputations shining, despite the fact that both as married men had liaisons with Marilyn Monroe, and in the case of J.F.K. several hundred other affairs. Much of the 'scandal' was reported after their deaths, and in retrospect considered insignificant compared with their achievements (it was only mindless bonking, after all). A magnetic personality is a great asset, for the public will forgive it many things. (Even Edward Kennedy has strangely survived the Chappaquiddick affair, though if he ever became a real contender for the Presidency, doubtless that old Chappa chestnut would be revived.)

The same cannot be said for Nixon and the Watergate scandal. Bugging the HQ of your political rivals is a more serious offence than the Kennedys' womanizing, simply because it is totally illegal, whereas adultery is not. At least in the West, that is. Nixon still retains some status today, however, as his political wisdom is still widely sought by senators and presidents alike.

No one could believe Ronald Reagan could be involved in the Iran-Contra affair, and so even though Ollie North might be a hero to some, Reagan will never enjoy the status of a scandal survivor.

When it comes to those individuals just below the ultimate seat of power, the verdict can go either way with a scandal. Gary Hart didn't survive his own particular one in America, whereas Cecil Parkinson in Britain did. Could he have had friends in even higher places watching over him?

Rock stars

These people's lifestyles have been renowned for outrage for so long that little they do nowadays is considered remotely scandalous. Yet P. J. Proby, a sixties crooner of a chart hit or two, had his whole career inadvertently wiped out when his trousers split on stage during a concert, while Jerry Lee Lewis was hounded from state to state in the late fifties for having a child bride. David Bowie does stand out for successfully capitalizing on his ambivalent sexuality in the seventies, at a time when certain sections of society were genuinely scandalized by it. The jury is still out with regard to the Elton John *Sun* 'exposé'. As for Bill Wyman and Mandy Smith? Well, he's a Stone, isn't he?

Movie stars
While the Fatty Arbuckle manslaughter/rape scandal was very prominent in its day and swiftly ended his career, many of Hollywood's biggest scandals were kept quiet. Kenneth Anger's *Hollywood Babylon* books reveal exactly how many scandals were hushed up by various studios and interested parties. Even Rock Hudson's private life was kept private until right at the end.

Business
Though involved in the Guinness scandal, Ivan Boesky survived his actions with consummate ease. Ernest Saunders, on the other hand, did not and is less likely to.

Religion
In an age of defrocked priests continuing their spiritual duties and women taking holy orders, it is only at the top end of the religious hierarchy that scandal creates waves. Two of the top TV evangelists in America, Bakker and Swaggart, are both in the doghouse for their extra-marital activities. But rumours are they intend to make a comeback.

Ex-Nazis
While it is doubtful whether Kurt Waldheim will ever recover from the stories of his nasty past, Herbert von Karajan's alleged membership of the Hitler Youth and Nazi Party seems not to have remotely affected any of his vast gramophone sales. 'I vos young, and didn't know any bedder.'

THE SCANDAL SURVIVOR'S AWARD: This goes to Jeffrey Archer, former Member of Parliament and bestselling author.

Criminal status

There are many criminals and outlaws who, despite their anti-social deeds, have attained great status with the rest of society as well as with their peers. If you're going for crime in a big way you may as well be Public Enemy No. 1, or 'the mastermind behind' or the 'greatest criminal mind of his generation', rather than simply a petty criminal.

Whereas a drug dealer doesn't have any status whatsoever (least of all in Singapore), a computer hacker (Kevin Mitnick, Hans Hubner), a famous forger (Clifford Irving and the Howard Hughes biography; the Hitler Diaries man), an insider trader (Ivan Boesky), a daring bank robber (the Frenchman Jacques Mesrine), a society cat burglar may have. Great escapers, no matter what their crime, are always held in high regard, notably Henri Charrière (Papillon).

Criminal status, will, of course, usually depend on the crime. In fiction, where once it used to be a requirement for criminals to get their just deserts, nowadays so long as the criminal act isn't too heinous they often get away with it. In reality, even a murderer can carry a degree of status if he evades detection long enough to catch the public interest, for example Dr Crippen, Sweeney Todd, Jack the Ripper.

NB: spending a night in the cells is something to brag about. In the same way, any person worth his or her salt has been fired (not sacked) at least once in their lives.

Going out in style – 'You'll never take me alive' gestures and Gary Gilmore's request for a firing squad execution ('Let's do it') – evoke similar degrees of status.

Some criminals and outlaws who had status
Colonel Thomas Blood – the only person ever to steal the Crown Jewels, get caught and be pardoned instead of executed by Charles II for his audacity

Robin Hood – one suspects that Robin wasn't the great guy he was made out to be, yet his reputation is unassailable

Billy the Kid – despite being a psychotic killer, he is a legendary figure of the old west

Jesse James – as above

Thomas Crown – after successfully carrying out a stylish bank robbery, he organized a carbon copy, equally successfully, just to prove a point

Ivan Boesky

The Kray Brothers (at least among their peers)
Raffles
Jack the Ripper
Moriarty (Sherlock Holmes's great rival)
John Dillinger – robbed more banks in one year than Jesse James
   did in sixteen. His Public Enemy No. 1 tag was richly deserved
Bonnie and Clyde
Al Capone
The Scarlet Pimpernel
William Tell
Butch and Sundance
Dick Turpin

Death status

The way in which you leave this world, or simply the sheer fact that you're deceased, can add to your status. Whether you're one of the lucky ones who receive status before you die, like the Japanese kamikaze pilot elite in the last war, or whether some time has to pass before the significance of your life and death is realized, like Vincent Van Gogh and a whole host of artists and musicians, status death does exist. The Unknown Soldier in several cathedrals around the world is hardly a well-known personality, but he is revered all the same.

Those who die bravely are accredited great status, as are great talents that die tragically young – Rupert Brooke (28), Thomas Chatterton (17), Joan of Arc (19), Schubert (31), Rudolph Valentino (31), Christopher Marlowe (29), Shelley (29), Keats (25), Aubrey Beardsley (25).

Cheating death confers possibly the greatest status of them all, since you end up living on. If you must dabble in the status of death, however, it's probably best to fake it, like Reginald Perrin.

Suicide status

Morbid though it may seem, suicides have been known to boost their perpetrator's standing in the community. The unseen hero,

Alex, of the film *The Big Chill* is a suicide who through his magnetism while alive has the power to draw all his close friends together for a weekend in the country following his funeral. Through his absence, they are brought to greater realization of, and closeness with, each other.

Yukio Mishima's suicide was the crowning event of his exceptionally tortured life (the subject also of a film, *Mishima*), and gave sinister weight to his artistic and intellectual achievements.

Sylvia Plath, the poetess, has also become a beacon for other tortured souls, and her poetry and one novel, *The Bell Jar* are bestsellers today.

Even if the subject is not prepared to actually finish himself off, those figures who seem to have 'a death wish', those reckless characters who live life to the full, die young and have a good-looking corpse – Keith Richards ('I ain't dead yet!'), Gerry Garcia ('Neither am I!'), Keith Moon ('I am'), Jimi Hendrix, Jack Kerouac, Neal Cassady, et al. (hold the bit about 'the good-looking corpse') – have a kind of status about them, since we would not choose to live their way, we still admire them.

Cads and bounders

Rogues, cads and bounders can be extremely lovable and may be forgiven many things, provided they have bags of charm and style, and you don't happen to be the injured party. Status is attributed to these persons because it's very difficult for even the smartest among us to emerge from a whole series of low-life exploits still smelling of roses. Cads and bounders will rely solely on their good looks, charm, and style for their redemption. They live by their wits. Meanwhile they are forever taking the gamble that their public will bend over backwards to forgive and forget. And that's quite a gamble to take.

Successful cads and bounders get the best of both worlds – the fruits of their exploits and glowing forgiveness – while we jealously wonder how they keep getting away with it and why we would be unable to get away with it ourselves. The fact that they get away with it, and we daren't or can't, gives them status.

Cads and bounders begin early in life. They leave the top off the toothpaste. They pull the limbs off dumb animals. They are forever playing practical, and often dangerous, jokes throughout their lives. They run away from home. The parable of the prodigal son in the Bible appeals to them and they ensure the fatted calf is always killed when they return. Cads and bounders drink. They cheat at cards. They cheat on their wives and girlfriends, husbands and boyfriends (and are invariably forgiven, or they wouldn't do it for long). They borrow money from close friends and rarely pay them back. They use up all their favours and more, and when all seems lost for them, when it looks as if the world is finally about to turn on them, they ignite their Paul Newman smiles and go and perform one simple good deed that redeems them.

Cads' and bounders' role models are many – from literature there are Martin Amis's heroes, Flashman from *Tom Brown's Schooldays* and later the humorous George Macdonald Fraser novels, Tom Jones from the eponymous Henry Fielding novel, James Steerforth and Uriah Heep from *David Copperfield*, Count Fosco from *The Woman in White*, Howard Kirk in *The History Man*, Sebastian Dangerfield in *The Ginger Man*, Dean Moriarty from *On the Road*.

From the movies they mirror the exploits of Terry-Thomas, or Paul Newman in his earlier films, Jack Nicholson in *Five Easy Pieces*, Harry Lime in *The Third Man*, John Belushi and Dan Aykroyd in *The Blues Brothers*, Michael Caine in *Alfie*, Albert Finney in *Saturday Night and Sunday Morning*, Jean Paul Belmondo in *Au Bout de Souffle*.

From comic books come the examples of Dennis the Menace and the Penguin and the Riddler from Batman, Lex Luther from Superman.

And cads and bounders study with alarming precision the early exploits of the Rolling Stones and Errol Flynn.

NB: it is very rare for a woman to be a cad or a bounder and get away with it, such is the sexist nature of our society. Wicked women are usually made to show remorse. For example, though James Mason's highwayman in *The Wicked Lady* comes off rather nobly at the end of the movie, for Margaret Lockwood there is no forgiveness for her wicked deeds. Even Cat Woman's wicked ways must succumb to Batman's goody-goody philosophy.

And Marlene Dietrich, as perfect an example of the female cad or bounder as ever graced the screen (*The Blue Angel*, *Catherine the Great*) had to lose her sense of fun, and her life, to James Stewart's moralizing hero in *Destry Rides Again*. Where are all those Raymond Chandleresque femmes fatales these days?

TOP STATUS

When everything is weighed up, when everyone and everything connected with your life, every bit of information, every act and action, is fed into the big status computer, why is it that some individuals come out ahead, a head and a couple of shoulders even, above the rest?

You've done your homework on status. You find it quite easy to score points. You can tell, despite your rare contact with the riff-raff and lower orders of this world, that whatever it is, you've got it. Alan Whicker told you so when he profiled you recently on his very exclusive TV programme. Prince Philip told you so over G&Ts after you received your recent knighthood. Dustin Hoffman grudgingly intimated as much after the Oscars. And Donald Trump is extremely keen to have you aboard the *Trump Princess* even if Ivana can't bear the sight of your new girlfriend.

Everyone you meet is desperate for you to have their babies. You haven't put a foot wrong since you appeared feet first into the world. You go through the right entrances at Ascot and make timely exits before the press arrive. Your hair might be grey, but your shoes never are.

Yet, forever, there seems to be someone else who by ways and sneaky means has come out somewhere in front of you; has been raised to a slightly higher plane; is sitting on a higher, whiter, puffier cloud than the one you're standing on. Like a Dante's Inferno in reverse.

So who are those guys and gals that outbid the highest bidder, that pip at the post, that pull out the stops? Who are these stage-managers of status who inhabit the rarefied planes of top status? More to the point, how do we mere mortals get up there?

Men who have achieved the top status award in the past

Top status awards are not given out every year. In fact, they tend
to be a very random affair and, often, given out posthumously.

1480: Leonardo da Vinci   1940: Winston Churchill
1805: Horatio Nelson   1942: Humphrey Bogart
1808: Lord Byron   1947: Gandhi
1900: Oscar Wilde   1953: Cecil Beaton
1935: T. E. Lawrence   1955: David Niven
   (Lawrence of Arabia)   1962: John Fitzgerald Kennedy
1936: Pablo Picasso   1980: John Lennon

Women who have achieved the top status award in the past

35 B.C.: Cleopatra   1918: Mata Hari
A.D. 50: Queen Boadicea   1920: Emmeline Pankhurst
1429: Joan of Arc   1956: Grace Kelly
1588: Queen Elizabeth I   1958: Marilyn Monroe
1745: Catherine the Great   1985: Mother Teresa of
1880: Florence Nightingale   Calcutta

The 1990 top status award – men

GIANNI AGNELLI (Italy): Boss of the Fiat motor company. More
famous than the Italian royal family, more revered than the Pope.
Loved by kings and commoners alike. Uncrowned prince of Italy.
From his hilltop villa near Turin at La Collina, an exclusive
enclave of the rich and famous, Agnelli heads a dynasty which is
the natural successor to the late Princes of Savoy. His business
skills are envied throughout the world, he is pressed by friends
and allies to don the mantle of international statesman-cum-
philosopher-king in the new Europe of 1992. His life is one long
list of triumphs and successes. He knows everyone and his
international status is without peer.

Current contenders (the short list)

ARMAND HAMMER (US): Oil magnate. Capitalist. One of the few living people to have met Lenin. Armand travels extensively and is vastly influential in world affairs. He has had the ear of several US and Soviet presidents. If he wins the award he will give away all his money.

HERBERT VON KARAJAN (Germany): Conductor of international repute. Headed the Berlin Philharmonic Orchestra. Survived the scandal of once being a member of the Nazi Party. Looked like an older version of Giorgio Armani. (Died in 1989, but eligible posthumously.)

FRANK SINATRA (US): Crooner, movie star, much married, highly respected charitable showbiz personality. Rumours of possible 'mob' connections, but like Karajan an escaper of serious scandals. Impeccable credentials. Long overdue for the top status award. If he wins the award he'll write a hit song about it.

ALAN WHICKER (GB): From his base on Whicker Island, Al makes his occasional forays into the world, meets everyone and makes a programme about them. He extracts the Michael mercilessly but everyone loves him for it. Wick is his own boss totally. A lousy dresser who gets away with it with consummate ease.

HORST P. HORST (Germany): A top fashion photographer since the thirties. Horst is still snapping the top anorexic beauties of the day. He is also well overdue for the award. If he wins it, he'll photograph it in black and white.

PRINCE CHARLES (GB): British aristocrat and part-time royal. Despite the fact that Charles could have wallowed in the easy life, he has gone against the code of mindless duty and voiced his opinions, often with great effect, against some of the crap that's going on around us. His Pater is furious, but he presses on regardless. He'll only accept the award if it's nicely designed.

SAMUEL BECKETT (Ireland): late writer. His new play *Waiting for the Status Award* was uncompleted at the time of his death. In the meantime, such is his status as a writer that he could have charged £1,000 for a thousand-word limited edition work, *Stirrings Still*, even if it was only to help out an old publisher friend. Beckett believed all awards to be absurd in the extreme, but he would have made an exception for this one. (Died in 1989, but eligible posthumously.)

J. D. SALINGER (US): Writer and recluse. Author of *The Catcher in the Rye*. J. D. recently came out of hiding to take legal action against a biography that was being written about him. An enigmatic character. We can only guess if he'd come out of hiding to receive the award if he won it.

THE REST WHO DIDN'T MAKE THE SHORT LIST: Arthur Miller (US), playwright and former husband of Marilyn Monroe; Rudolf Nureyev (USSR), ballet dancer; Sir Karl Popper (GB), philosopher; Clint Eastwood (US), actor and potential future US President; John Peel (GB), disc jockey; Lord Weidenfeld (GB), publisher; Robert De Niro (US), actor; Sir James Goldsmith (GB), business tycoon; David Attenborough (GB), nature person; the Dalai Lama (Tibet), religious leader.

The 1990 top status award – women

Jointly won by Catherine Deneuve, French actress, and Tina Brown, British editor of the US magazine *Vanity Fair*.

Catherine is possibly one of the most celebrated women in the whole of France. Bright, intellectual and beautiful, many still see her in one of her more famous roles in Luis Buñuel's *Belle de Jour* (1967) as the bored Parisian housewife who goes on the game in the afternoons to while away the time. Though a swinging sixties lady and former Mrs David Bailey, Catherine always retained her sense of Euro style and cultured outlook. Nowadays she makes few celluloid appearances and spends more time with her family. Her most recent international film was *The Hunger* with David Bowie.

Tina Brown is the archetypal whizz-kid magazine editor. What Citizen Kane was to the newspaper world, she is to magazine journalism, but with greater success. Not only did she turn around the floundering society mag *Tatler*, and turn it into one of the brightest successes of the decade, she has had a similar success with the American *Vanity Fair* which suffered from similar problems.

Married to Harold Evans, former Editor of the *Sunday Times*, she works in Manhattan and spends weekends at her Long Island base.

The runners-up

VANESSA REDGRAVE: One of the great independent English actresses, one-time Trotskyite and activist in radical politics. Many liken her to an English version of Jane Fonda. Vanessa is mother to Joely and Natasha Richardson, both successful actresses in their own right. Still acting.

MRS THATCHER: Alias Supernanny, Matron and The Iron Lady. No one inspires more contrary feelings of dislike and affection than our Maggie. An incarnation of Boadicea and good Queen Bess, one way or another she has transformed England into a nation economically more prosperous (for some) and respected, if not a happier one.

ANNA FORD: TV presenter and one-time news anchorperson, Anna together with the late Marc Boxer (former Editor of the *Tatler* and cartoonist) were a true status couple. Reputed not to take any nonsense from anyone, Anna once threw a glass of wine over Jonathan Aitken, head of TV-AM.

DIANE SAWYER: US newscaster and a modern American classic. Successful, brainy and beautiful. Men want to marry her, women want to be her. America is in love with her. She has been likened to Grace Kelly.

JERRY HALL: American super model. Rich, independent, successful in her own right. Unmarried trouble and strife to Mick. Universally feared 'leg-wrestler'.

ILONA STALLER (Italy) 'La Cicciolina': Italian porno star and genuinely elected member of the government.

NANCY REAGAN: Ronnie's wife. One-time power behind the throne. One-time most influential first lady. Still very influential among power-brokers and 'ladies who lunch'.

ANITA RODDICK: Founder of The Body Shop cosmetics chain worth over £30 million. Turned down by all sorts of financial institutions at first, her gritty determination won through and the company was floated in the early 1980s.

THE BEST OF THE REST: Meryl Streep (US), actress; Jane Fonda (US), actress and political activist; Jean Muir (GB), fashion designer; Shirley Maclaine (US), actress and novelist; Raisa Gorbachev (USSR), first lady; Clare Booth Luce (US), socialite, journalist, politician, stateswoman; the Queen Mum (GB); Joan Collins (GB), actress, superstar; Charlotte Rampling (GB), actress.

Two things to remember about top status

1. You have to be voted top status, either by other people with TS or the all-powerful public. You can't vote yourself up to that rarefied, higher plane. So exit stage left Derek Hatton, General Galtieri, Andrew Ridgely, Terry Wogan, Noel Edmonds, Bruce Willis, Peter Stringfellow, Kylie Minogue, Bros, Jonathan Ross, Patrick Lichfield, Jimmy Tarbuck, Imelda Marcos, and Saddam Hussein.

2. Top status is not guaranteed for life.

Waning top status: Duran Duran, the over-exposed photographer Helmut Newton, Bianca Jagger, Paloma 'I've dined out on my Daddy's surname for too long now' Picasso, the 'palimony' divorce lawyer Marvin Mitchelson (who made a name for himself by defending the rich and famous against their even more rich and famous spouses), J. R. Ewing (there are only so many times he can be shot, stabbed and firebombed to boost the soap's flagging ratings) and Ian 'there must be more to life than *A Question of Sport*' Botham.

Lost top status: Worse than the waning variety. Those who once had top status but then lost it completely include the late Orson Welles, one-time top City businessman Jim 'asset stripper' Slater, Dudley 'I should have stayed in Britain' Moore, David 'It's about time I recorded a hit album' Bowie, Henry 'there's never a Nixon scandal around when you want one' Kissinger, David Frost, George Best and Ernest Saunders (ex-Guinness chairman).

Don't despair, however. Lost top status can be found again. Welcome back Cliff Richard, G. Gordon Liddy, George Harrison.

Some ways mere mortals can achieve top status

HAVING

Time
Absolute privacy
Health
Good looks
A private income
A serious hardback biography
  written about you
Several serious hardback
  biographies written about
  you (there's always a new
  and contentious angle of
  your life that hasn't been
  explored)
Your own personal tailor and
  shoemaker
Your *Times* obituary already
  written, and constantly
  updated
An analyst in Vienna

NOT HAVING

A street named after you or a
  park bench, but a whole city
  (for example Leningrad,
  Sydney)

GIVING

Speeches to the United
  Nations
Multiple orgasms

CHEATING

Death (difficult)
The Inland Revenue
  (impossible)

WINNING

The Americas Cup
The last hand of the biggest
  poker game in the universe

FULFILLING

A childhood dream
An impossible ambition

BEING

First to do a particular thing
  (like climb a mountain)
A famous artist in your own
  lifetime (Bacon, Warhol,
  Hockney, Dali)
Accepted equally by two
  opposed cultures (Armand
  Hammer who has the ear of
  East and West)
On *Desert Island Discs*
There at the right time
An honorary member of the
  Tina Chow Set

KNOWING

When to quit while you're
  ahead
Exactly what to say at the right
  time (never having to regret
  'I wish I had said that then')

DISCOVERING

The meaning of life

STATUS IN THE FUTURE

In an ever-changing world, future status is difficult to predict. After all, it's difficult enough keeping up with status in the present without having to invest in the future as well. Yet he or she who anticipates status successfully will put themselves further and further beyond the reach of their status-seeking competitors.

Films and books that deal with the future may give us a guideline as to what to expect. In Ridley Scott's classic futuristic thriller *Blade Runner* the object seems to be to own things that are real rather than synthetic, like a pet owl, or a performing snake, and have memories and photographs to assure you that you were human and not a genetically engineered android. In the film, large bureaucratic multinational organizations are the employers of the future, so it might be as well to start climbing that corporate ladder now.

In Woody Allen's *Sleeper* the status symbols of those leading a leisured, privileged existence appear to be cybernetic servants to wait on you hand and well-manicured foot; an orgasmatron for automatic mechanical sexual gratification (far too vulgar actually to perform sex with a partner); and a highly potent drug, Orb, which was passed around after a dinner party in place of the port bottle.

In the film *Soylent Green*, the vision of the future is one of over-population and overcrowding. So in exchange for your body, which is painlessly exterminated and served up as human fodder, you are permitted to view the most fabulous vision accessible only to the few: a piece of rare and highly emotional film footage of the way things once were – green fields, streams, trees, unpolluted skies – the natural world that is fast disappearing today. Status in this future would seem to involve owning some uninfected green-belt land, or more simply a solitary house plant.

The theme of violence in the future seems to be a common one, as in *A Clockwork Orange*. With law and order barely able to cope, it would seem we would need a *Robocop*. Status, in this particular future vision, was having sufficient funds to protect yourself from the baddies, owning a tank instead of a car, and some hand-held easily-launched heat-seeking missiles.

Both Orwell's *1984* and Huxley's *Brave New World* deal with future dictatorships, cruel or benevolent, where you are either little people, or someone high up and powerful in the bureaucracy. In the case of *Brave New World*, the current class system is extended into a wide system of gradings where your lifetime's status is predetermined chemically, not from the womb, but straight from the test tube. So unless you've got some influence at the sperm bank, status in these cases is based completely on luck.

Most themes dealing with the future suggest that the most difficult facet of life will be maintaining a mind of your own in the dictatorships of the future. In the advent of these, degrees of power and freedom will become the ultimate status symbols. As well as a mind of your own, of course.

Hopefully, we will be spared from a Big Brother vision of the future. If we are, and no great revolutions or upheavals affect us, then future status can be largely determined by many of the things that are happening in the world today. These will be governed by four main factors: the environment factor, the economy factor, the medical advances factor, and, most significantly, the Ayatollah factor.

THE PROPERTY MARKET: With the advent of the Channel Tunnel, people are already beginning to buy second and third homes in Normandy and Brittany. Clever thinking. But what about buying further afield? With glasnost and perestroika becoming even more prevalent, the Berlin Wall come down and Eastern Europe opening up, why not look that bit further for that second Chez Nous or Mon Repos? Instead of Neuchâtel why not East Berlin? Why not go all the way to Leningrad or Moscow? The property is still cheap and the potential fantastic.

TRAVEL: 'Guess what, everybody. I've just come back from a holiday on the Sea of Tranquillity.'

'Yeah, well, not only have we seen the Rings of Saturn, pal, we've also visited two entirely new dimensions on a Club Black Holes holiday.'

It is in fact possible to book the Space Shuttle now, so status in the future, travel-wise, will still be a possibility. It's just that it won't be on the planet earth, that's all.

In the shorter term, there are plenty of horses for when the oil runs out. And plenty of bicycles for when the horses run out. So travel will always be possible.

LEARNING TO FLY: In the same way that we all drive a car today, in the future many of us will need to fly. The earlier the better. And if you can get some space-ship lessons in, you'll go even further.

POLITICS: Green.

THE ARTS: Invest in the current talent of today; young painters and writers. With the abject unoriginality of movie plots nowadays, start buying the rights to great first novels with filmic potential. Aim by 1995 to have your own studio.

In TV and Radio there's likely to be a marked increase in the number of stations and channels, whether Italian housewives do it on TV or not. So many more people will enjoy the status of having their own radio programme or chat show, with the result that this status will diminish.

BUSINESS: Buy nebulous shares in Mars, Jupiter and other future off-world colonies if you want your future family to be influential in the Universe. You, of course, will be branded a loony and unfortunately won't live to see their success. Once again, over the shorter term, there is great potential now for a green economy, for example acid rain resistant roofs and headgear, fresh water, air filters, solar powered roll-on deodorants, unleaded loos, Beauty without Cruelty.

THE HOME: Security, privacy, space, quiet, neighbours at least two miles away.

FOOD: 'Hey, I bought an organically grown vegetable at the greengrocer this morning. Pretty amazing individual, aren't I?'

'The Picasso? We took it down from above the fireplace. I think the free-range egg box looks much nicer. It certainly cost enough.'

Put wine and port down now. Great future status symbols. 1980, '81, '82, '83, '85, '86, '89 are all excellent years and still relatively cheap.

WEALTH/INVESTMENT: In the shorter term, the first person to buy a share that actually goes up instead of down will receive great status. In the future, the first person to become a trillionaire will catch some admiring glances. Then it's a question of gold, precious stone and plutonium millionaires instead of paper money ones.

ULTIMATE FUTURE STATUS SYMBOL: The elixir of life?

MISCELLANEOUS STATUS

NIGHTCLUBS: Not visiting them.

GENTLEMAN'S CLUBS: Being a member of one, e.g. White's, Boodle's, Brook's (London). The Union, The Brook, The River (New York). The Bel Air Bay Club (Los Angeles). The Bohemian Club (San Francisco). The Metropolitan Club (Washington DC).

CASINOS: Aspinall's (London).

TELEVISION: Not owning a TV is high status.

READING: Finishing and enjoying *Gravity's Rainbow* by Thomas Pynchon.

SURVIVING: A plane crash. A scandal. More than one round with Mike Tyson.

BEING: Quoted. Fired (as opposed to being made redundant). A name at Lloyd's. A good shot. A black belt. A contender. 'Unlike other men and women.'

NOT BEING: Receptive to hypnotism.

HAVING: A mistress or a toyboy. An antique four-poster bed. An IQ rating in excess of Bernard Levin's. A Swiss bank account. Breakfast at Tiffany's and tea at the Ritz. A rare blood group.

DRINKING: Out of China teacups. A boorish lout under the table.

GETTING: Robert De Niro to make a cameo appearance in your film.

SHOPPING: In New Bond Street as opposed to Knightsbridge.

COMPLETING: The hardest crossword on the journey to or from work.

THROWING: A stone into the sea further than anyone else.

SCORING: A century in cricket.

IDENTIFYING: A classical music piece without hearing the opening bars.

MAINTAINING: Your composure under extreme pressure. An erection.

PAINTING: A masterpiece.

Index